ENCOUNTERS
WITH JESUS

Forty days in the life of Jesus
through the eyes
of those HE touched.

By Benjamin Nelson

Cover Art:

I Shall Be Whole
(The Woman with an Issue of Blood)
Painted by Al Young

Used with kind permission from Al Young Studios
www.alyoung.com

Cover and Text Design: Christopher Nelson
csnelsondesign.com

Editor: Susan Hughes
MyIndependentEditor.com

Scripture taken from *The Message*. Copyright © 1993, 1994, 1995, 1996, 2000, 2001, 2002. Used by permission of NavPress Publishing Group.

Another Red Letter Day Publishing
Westwood, NJ

AnotherRedLetterDay.com

ISBN 13: 978-0-6924-0350-1

ISBN 10: 0-6924-0350-7

Contents

PASSION

RESURRECTION

ACKNOWLEDGMENTS

I want to say thank you to some folks.

My first thank you goes to my wife who looked at me while we were out to dinner with our home fellowship group and said, "You could write a book." I said, "Okay, I will." Then she loved me through the many times I asked if I could read to her, or asked what she thought of this or that. I love you Corinna!

Next to my dear friend, Larry Carroll, who has encouraged me along the way, trying desperately to keep me on the straight and narrow of English grammar and punctuation.

Thanks also to my wonderful editor, Susan Hughes. Her attention to detail and knowledge of her craft amaze me.

Thanks to my son Chris whose keen eye for design can be seen on every page of this work.

And special thanks to my blogging community for all your caring feedback and constant encouragement. It has kept me writing. You're all such an amazing blessing.

Clearly, the one who really deserves praise and thanks and honor is Jesus, my favorite topic. I would say it was all Him and none of me, but if that were the case, the book would be much better.

Lord Jesus, You are worthy of all honor and glory. All praise is due You.

Bless the Lord, O my soul, and all that is within me bless His holy name.

INTRODUCTION

I love stories. I love to hear them, and I love to tell them. It's what we do in the Nelson family. Any time we're sitting around the living room or dinner table with friends or family, we're telling stories. Some of the stories we tell have been told a hundred times, but we still tell them, embellishing all the right parts and forgetting those embarrassing details. But it's no use trying to pretend you didn't break that bowl, set fire to the carpet, or wander off and get lost at that park. Someone at the table will remember.

Jesus was a storyteller. He used stories to teach about the kingdom of God. He used stories to convict and convince. He used stories to help us draw conclusions and to leave us scratching our heads.

The Lord saw fit to fill His Word with narratives—stories—to teach us the wisdom of the ages. We have the stories of ancient Israel. We learn of their victories and their defeats. We learn about great men of faith like Daniel, Noah, Job, David, and Elijah. We learn of villains like Ahab and Jezebel, Sanballat, Sennacherib, and Nabal. We see the good side of folks and their bad side as well.

So when I read the Gospels, I see stories inside the stories. I wonder what it would have been like to be there and see Jesus heal a blind man or cast out the devil. What would it have been like to hear Him say "Hush!" to the storm or to have Him reject you as unfit for the kingdom of God?

This volume contains forty such stories, forty encounters with Jesus. In each I take on the voice of a character from scripture. Some Jesus touched; others observe Him at a distance; each is impacted by his or her encounter with Him. They are not meant to replace scripture, and there are times I make bold leaps into fiction. They each have some basis in the Gospels. The stories are arranged chronologically, for the most part, though some cover a period of years, and others express a story inferred by one verse in the text.

I pray that as you read these short vignettes from the lives of those who crossed paths with the Messiah, you will be drawn to the Word and to Jesus Himself. I hope they will cause you to think about these stories from a different perspective. My aim is to help everyone who reads them to consider Him anew.

I suggest you don't sit down and read right through, but that you take one story a day for forty days. Read the story and then read the Bible passage it comes from. See what the Spirit speaks to your heart as you do. You may see Jesus through new eyes.

Finally, I want to thank you for taking the time to read this work. I hope you encounter Jesus in these pages.

INCARNATION

He will herald God's arrival in the style and strength of Elijah,
soften the hearts of parents to children,
and kindle devout understanding among
hardened skeptics—he'll get the people ready for God.
Luke 1:17

THE PRAYER I NO LONGER PRAY

ZACHARIAH

We always wanted to have children. My dear Elizabeth and I both came from large families. We understood the blessings of many siblings. We could both trace our roots back to the house of Aaron in the tribe of Levi. I had been a priest for forty years. Any son of mine would follow in fifteen-hundred-year-old footsteps to serve in the temple.

When my father first told me I would marry Liza, I was a bit disappointed. She was much younger than me. But during our betrothal year, we got to know one another, and I saw that it was a good match. Even then, in those early days, our love grew.

We both loved the Almighty One and felt the honor of serving in the temple. Of course, our service took different forms. I helped prepare the temple for the holy days. I arranged for the wood and oil needed and coordinated the supplies with the vendors who sold to the temple.

She served with the administration and distribution of food and alms for the poor. It seems the poor always found their way to this holy city.

We hoped to start our family on our wedding night, but it was not to be. At first we thought nothing of it, but after two years of wanting children and having none, my Liza began to wonder. Was the Almighty punishing us? Why would our heavenly Father withhold this greatest of all blessings from His own children?

We prayed and made many special offerings. Many days we fasted and cried out to the Lord for His mercy.

Without a firstborn to offer up to the Lord, we felt as though we could never please Him.

Liza and I agreed to fast one day every week until God heard our prayer and gave us a child. But as the weeks turned to years and the years wore on, still the heavens were silent. The doctors could find nothing wrong, and we began to fear the worst.

When the doctor said the word barren, it was as though something snapped inside my wife.

I don't think she was ever truly happy after that. She wasn't moping about or crying all the time, but the light I'd seen in young Liza's eyes on our wedding day—the light of hope, of expectation—that part of Liza died with the speaking of that word.

Finally, we stopped praying, stopped asking, stopped hoping for a child. We continued to serve God the best we could; we just knew we would never have the joy of raising a child. Our family would stop with me. Our brothers and sisters were growing families, and we were just growing old.

That year, I drew the lot to work in the holy place offering incense. It was a huge honor that many priests never know. The incense we offered represented the prayers of His people rising before His throne. Though Liza and I had stopped hoping for a child, stopped seeking the Lord for the miracle of birth in our family, I was still thrilled at the prospect of serving this way.

The day arrived and I put on my linen garments. They tied the cord around my ankle so they could retrieve my body if I offended the Holy One. I made my way through the immense curtain into the Holy of Holies, incense in hand. As I entered, I sensed something different. The difference was not in the temple furniture or adornment. It was not in the smell of the incense. It was in me.

Was it hope rising up in me? That didn't make any sense. Not only was Liza barren, she was past the time of women. She had been that way for years now. But why should I hope? As I neared the altar of incense, my hopefulness grew stronger.

Suddenly, as I prepared to offer the incense, an angel appeared just to the right of the altar. I dropped the bowl I carried, and an explosion of fragrance diffused the glow that came from this being. As I started to fall to my knees, shaking from the inside out, the angel stopped me.

"Don't fear, Zachariah. Your prayer has been heard. Elizabeth, your wife, will bear a son by you. You are to name him John. You're going to leap like a gazelle for joy, and not only you—many will delight in his birth. He'll achieve great stature with God.

3

"He'll drink neither wine nor beer. He'll be filled with the Holy Spirit from the moment he leaves his mother's womb. He will turn many sons and daughters of Israel back to their God. He will herald God's arrival in the style and strength of Elijah, soften the hearts of parents to children, and kindle devout understanding among hardened skeptics—he'll get the people ready for God."

I could not believe my ears! The Father had heard the prayer I'd stopped praying. How could this be? I said to the angel, "Do you expect me to believe this? I'm an old man, and my wife is an old woman."

Though he told me not to be afraid, the look on his face made my knees tremble.

He said, "I am Gabriel, the sentinel of God, sent especially to bring you this glad news. But because you won't believe me, you'll be unable to say a word until the day of your son's birth. Every word I've spoken to you will come true on time—God's time."

I started to object, to recant, but I couldn't speak. My mouth worked just fine, but no sound came out.

It was then that I felt a tugging on the cord around my ankle. Those in the outer court were beginning to worry, since I'd been in there far longer than expected. I looked down at my ankle, and the light in the room dimmed. Gabriel was gone just as suddenly as he'd come.

When I finally emerged, everyone crowded around me. They had heard the voices and knew something happened. I made gestures, and they saw that I couldn't speak.

Once I finished my temple duties, I headed back home. At first Liza did not want to hope, but it was not too long after I returned home that she began to sense the change in her body.

When she began to show, we moved out of the city to a family home further from the crowds and neighbors. There we lived in wonder and amazement at how the Lord was answering our prayer—in His time and for His purposes. We were, for the most part, alone for the first five months. Then Elizabeth's young cousin, Mary, came to visit with the news that she was also with child.

Before she got the news out of her mouth, our little one leapt inside Elizabeth's womb. Mary told us of her encounter with Gabriel, and we all wondered at the mighty hand of the Lord on us.

As the day of Liza's delivery approached, Mary headed back to her home in Nazareth to be with her betrothed, Joseph. Liza and I awaited John's arrival.

What excitement surrounded his birth! All our friends and family showered us with love and blessings. On the eighth day, we took him to the rabbi for circumcision. The rabbi was about to announce him as Zachariah, as custom dictates.

Liza protested. "His name must be John!"

After some dispute, I gestured for a tablet, as I was still unable to speak of the matter. I wrote, his name is John.

At that instant, the Lord restored my voice. What could I do but praise the Holy One? What a day we lived in! What would become of this boy, and what of this baby Mary carried?

As I praised the Lord, His Spirit rose up within me and gave me these words:

"Blessed be the Lord, the God of Israel; He came and set his people free. He set the power of salvation in the center of our lives, and in the very house of David His servant, Just as He promised long ago through the preaching of His holy prophets: Deliverance from our enemies and every hateful hand; Mercy to our fathers, as He remembers to do what He said He'd do, What He swore to our father Abraham— a clean rescue from the enemy camp, So we can worship Him without a care in the world, made holy before Him as long as we live.

"And you, my child, 'Prophet of the Highest,' will go ahead of the Master to prepare His ways, Present the offer of salvation to His people, the forgiveness of their sins. Through the heartfelt mercies of our God, God's Sunrise will break in upon us, Shining on those in the darkness, those sitting in the shadow of death, Then showing us the way, one foot at a time, down the path of peace."

What amazing times are upon us!

~~~

To read the original story, see Luke 1:5-25, 57-80.

5

*"Yes, I see it all now: I'm the Lord's maid, ready to serve.
Let it be with me just as you say."*
Luke 1:38

Do as You See Fit

Mary

I have always loved the Lord Almighty. I know you look at a young girl like me and suspect the worst. You see my condition and think you know everything about me. You see an unwed girl great with child, though barely old enough to conceive. I understand, but will you at least listen to my story?

In our home, dinnertime meant story time. Every night my father would tell us the stories of our great God. Stories filled with miracles and wonders. Stories of deliverance and rescue. Since there were four of us girls in the house, he would be sure to tell us of the wonderful Hebrew women. He wanted us to understand that Jehovah loved women and could use them to fulfill His purposes. He told us of Esther and Rahab, of Jael and Deborah, Rebecca and Rachel.

My father loved to talk of our lineage, especially that we could trace our family all the way back to King David. He liked to say we had royal blood. I loved the Sabbath, because we would walk through town to the synagogue as a family—arm in arm, all together. My father would say he was taking his princesses to the house of the King. But those days are gone.

When he learned I was pregnant he cut me off. I was no longer welcome at the dinner table. He would not be seen in the streets with me. He would not have me beneath his roof. He used to say he was sure the Lord had big plans for me, his princess, but now he considers me a disgrace. He says I have dragged both the Lord's name and his into the filth. He won't even let me tell him my story, but I hope you will listen.

When I was younger, my father promised me to an older man, Joseph the carpenter. Joseph was a good man and would often join us around the table. The month I first showed the signs of womanhood, they made our engagement official. There was an announcement in the square and a celebration in Joseph's home. By our custom, the engagement would last a year and then we would marry.

Oh how I looked forward to our wedding! I'd been dreaming of my wedding since my Aunt Rebecca's beautiful day. Never had I imagined such a celebration: the food, the singing and dancing, the joy, and oh the clothes! Once, my mother showed me the gown she wore on her wedding day, and she told me it would be altered to fit me someday. Not a month passed that I did not sneak into the back room to look at it. Sometimes I pulled it out of the chest where my mother kept it and danced around the room with it gripped tight against me.

Just two months after our engagement, I awoke with a start. There in my bedchamber stood a being. It terrified me. What was a man doing in my chamber? How did he get here? What did he want? Was he here to hurt me? I began to tremble. Then he spoke to me.

"Good morning! You're beautiful with God's beauty, beautiful inside and out! God be with you. Mary, you have nothing to fear. God has a surprise for you: You will become pregnant and give birth to a son and call his name Jesus. He will be great, be called 'Son of the Highest.' The Lord God will give him the throne of his father David; He will rule Jacob's house forever—no end, ever, to his kingdom."

This confused me further. On the eve of my engagement, my father sat down with me and explained how pregnancy and birth would happen. He did not want me to be afraid of Joseph. I knew my children would be born from a place of intimacy with my husband, born of our love. But Joseph and I had not been intimate. We had never even been alone together; my father had seen to that.

"But how? I've never known a man in that way," I blurted out.

The angel was not put off by my question nor did he seem surprised that I asked it. He sat down on the edge of my bed and said:

"The Holy Spirit will come upon you, the power of the Highest hover over you; Therefore, the child you bring to birth will be called Holy, Son of God.

"And did you know that your cousin Elizabeth conceived a son, old as she is? Everyone called her barren, and here she is six months pregnant! Nothing, you see, is impossible with God."

I sat in wonder and remembered all the women before me who had served God and put their lives in His hands. Suddenly, I saw it all so clearly. I was the Lord's maid, and I was ready and eager to serve Him.

That day, I didn't know how much it would cost. I didn't realize how much would be taken from me: my sisters and brothers, my father and mother, my place in the community of faith. These I would offer up as a sacrifice to carry this Holy One.

Within a month my mother knew I was pregnant, and she told my father. He put me out. Joseph, too, was going to disavow our engagement, until he had an encounter of his own. After talking it over, we decided it was best for me to stay with my cousin, Elizabeth.

We made the trip to the home of Zachariah and my Aunt Liza. I called her Aunt Liza because she was so much older than me, far too old to be with child.

I always loved trips out to the country, but it was not the same in the first stages of pregnancy.

"Aunt Liza!" I called out as we arrived in their yard.

Upon hearing my voice, Elizabeth ran to the door. When she saw me, both of us felt our children—our boys—tumble within us. It was as though they were connected. I so needed that confirmation! I had not imagined the whole thing. I know that sounds foolish, since I felt the confirmation inside me every day. But to see Liza, to feel that connection—it was exactly what I needed.

She ran to me as best she could and declared over me:

"You're so blessed among women, and the babe in your womb, also blessed! And why am I so blessed that the mother of my Lord visits me? The moment the sound of your greeting entered my ears, the babe in my womb skipped like a lamb for sheer joy. Blessed woman, who believed what God said, believed every word would come true!"

Then the Spirit welled up in me and I began to almost sing!

"I'm bursting with God-news; I'm dancing the song of my Savior God. God took one good look at me, and look what happened— I'm the most fortunate woman on earth! What God has done for me will never be forgotten, the God whose very name is holy, set apart from all others. His mercy flows in wave after wave on those who are in awe before him. He bared his arm and showed his strength, scattered the bluffing braggarts. He knocked tyrants off their high horses, pulled victims out of the mud. The starving poor sat down to a banquet; the callous rich were left out in the cold. He embraced his chosen child, Israel; he remembered and piled on the mercies, piled them high. It's exactly what he promised, beginning with Abraham and right up to now."

I don't know what will become of me, but I know the Almighty is with me–in me. The Lord is doing a great thing, a great thing in me, a great thing in Israel, a great thing in this world.

I don't care what else it costs me. I know the Lord is in this, and I long for the day I deliver this Holy Child.

~~~

To read the original story, see Luke 1:26-56.

"She will bring a son to birth, and when she does, you,
Joseph, will name Him Jesus—'God saves'—because
He will save his people from their sins."
Matthew 1:21

TAKE THIS WOMAN

JOSEPH

Have you ever been so angry you couldn't think about anything else? Every time you tried to do your work, you found your mind going back to your anger like your tongue searching for a chipped tooth.

That's where it all started for me.

That first afternoon after Mary came to my shop and told me she was pregnant, I ruined two chairs and had to start over on an order that was already late. At first I could only feel pain. Hurt. Cut to the core. I'd been betrayed. In short order, it all turned to anger.

I thought about the law. I wouldn't be the first good Jew to accuse his betrothed and turn her over to the council for punishment. But the law was so harsh: public stoning. I didn't have it in me to do that to Mary. My mind painted a picture of the two of us standing alone in the market square—me with stone in hand and her on her knees, praying for mercy. Then I was weeping. I was fond of her. Had you asked me that morning, I would have said I loved her, but with this . . . this betrayal, this deception . . . I didn't know what to think.

My trade is carpentry, and I take pride in my workmanship. When I commit to having a table and chairs ready for the Sabbath, I have it ready.

The afternoon she came to me and told me the unbelievable story about an angel and a visitation by the Holy One Himself, I couldn't keep my mind on my work. The anger rose, and I smashed my thumb and then shattered the chair leg I was turning.

It took me all night to finish that last chair for the set. It was already the fifth day, and Ari Bentamas would be here to pick up his order at the third hour.

I finally got it right just before dawn. I always tested each chair by sitting in it. I felt for places where the chair pressed or poked uncomfortably, checked to see if it wobbled. When I landed in the fourth chair, my fatigue won me over, and I fell into a deep sleep.

I dreamed I was back in the square again, a fist-sized stone in my grip. This time there was a mob watching me on both sides, as though I was the only one with a stone. They called out to me.

"Kill her!"

"Kill the harlot! She deserves to die!"

"She betrayed you."

"She betrayed the Almighty One."

They were spitting vile names at her, too: Whore, Filth, Jezebel.

Then, in the dream, someone walked up from behind me and stood at my side. He put his hand on the stone I was holding, and that was when I turned to look at him. He was radiant. He said:

"Joseph, son of David, don't hesitate to get married. Mary's pregnancy is Spirit-conceived. God's Holy Spirit has made her pregnant. She will bring a son to birth, and when she does, you, Joseph, will name him Jesus—'God saves'—because he will save his people from their sins."

I awoke to a banging on my shop door. The sun was up, and Ari had arrived to pick up his table and chairs. As I helped him load them into his cart, I thought about my dream. It was no fleeting dream that vanished like a vapor as I awoke. I could still hear his voice—the voice of that angel—telling me God's Holy Spirit had made Mary pregnant.

Once Ari was on his way home, I closed up shop and headed to see the rabbi. Seeing me at his door at that hour startled him, but when he saw my excitement he invited me in.

"What can I do for you, my son?" he asked.

I decided to get right to it.

"Isn't there something in the Prophets about a virgin being with child?" I asked.

He pondered this a bit and then went over to his scrolls.

"It seems to me there is something near the beginning of Isaiah's prophesies that mentions such a thing. Let me see. It was after Isaiah found himself in the throne room of the Lord Almighty. Ah! Here it is. It's just a brief mention. I never really thought about it, but it says:

'So the Master is going to give you a sign anyway. Watch for this: A girl who is presently a virgin will get pregnant. She'll bear a son and name him Immanuel (God-With-Us).'"

"Thank you, teacher," I said as I hugged the startled elder. Then I ran out of his house.

I ran straight to Mary's home and banged on the door. It took everything in me just to stand still while I waited for it to open. The Lord God was using Mary and me to bring His own Messiah to His people!

When she came to the door, I picked her up and spun her around on the steps.

"He came and told me, too! It's all true! I'm sorry I doubted you. The Lord is so wonderful!"

She began to cry, as did I. We were laughing and crying and dancing.

God has taken the worst thing that could ever happen to me and brought me my greatest joy. The crushing hurt I thought would kill me has turned to life and hope.

What a day! What a wonderful day!

~~~

To read the original story, see Matthew 1:18-25.

"A Savior has just been born in David's town,
a Savior who is Messiah and Master.
This is what you're to look for: a baby
wrapped in a blanket and lying in a manger."
Luke 2:11-12

Good News

Shepherds

"Where are we going, you ask? Didn't you see the sky light up to the south, just two leagues down the road toward Tekoa?"

I tend my sheep with a band of shepherds. We migrate from hillside to valley all around Jerusalem. My home is further north near Bethel, but we move our flocks often, always looking for the best pastures.

Our flock numbers about 600 at this time of year. In a few short months we will be selling off the best of them to the temple merchants for Passover. Meanwhile, we have to keep them out of trouble. If they're injured or marred in any way, the temple merchants won't buy them. We get a much better price from those who seek lambs for sacrifice than we do from those who want their wool and even less from the butchers.

Some despise shepherds or simply mock us. Some consider us lower than slaves. Often I receive less respect than the sheep I tend. But not tonight! I am still working through it in my mind.

Have you ever stepped out of total darkness into the full light of day? That's what it's like tonight as we set about our nightly watch.

Of course it's rarely completely dark on the Judean hillside. The Almighty One set such an array of lights in the sky! Sometime I think He did it just for us shepherds. As I look into the stars, I remember God's promise to Father Abraham. God told him to count the stars. I've tried that. The longer I look, the more stars seem to appear.

Even though the night was clear, with the moon and stars in their full glory, the brightness that lit the hillside washed it all away. It was brighter than the full sun of noonday. You can imagine the terror I felt. I was fully awake, part of me ready to fight and part of me ready to run.

A man stood in the midst of the field and called to us:

"Don't be afraid."

That's easy for him to say, but I move closer.

"I've come to announce joyful news meant for all people, everywhere."

With every step toward the being, I sense peace. I didn't know what it was, but it didn't seem dangerous.

"A Savior has just been born in David's town, a Savior who is Messiah and Master. This is what you're to look for: a baby wrapped in a blanket and lying in a manger."

David's town? He must be talking about Bethlehem, where King David—that shepherd turned King of Israel—was born.

At that, the brightness that surrounded us materialized into an army of angels, thousands on every side. No, not an army. A choir. The hillside rang out with all the voices of heaven singing:

"Glory to God in the heavenly heights, Peace to all men and women on earth who please him."

And then it was dark, all but one light to the north.

Now, I know the stars, and this one was new. It looked as though the heavenly host that had surrounded us minutes before had moved up to Bethlehem.

That's where we're headed now. Won't you come and see this Messiah, this Savior, with us?

~~~

To read the original story, see Luke 2:8-19.

"With my own eyes I've seen your salvation;
it's now out in the open for everyone to see:
A God-revealing light to the non-Jewish nations,
and of glory for your people Israel."
Luke 2:30-32

NOW I CAN GO

SIMEON

My father always said I should have been born a Levite. Even as a young boy, I loved the days we spent in the temple. I grew up just outside the holy city, so on Sabbath we would all go to the temple to gather for prayers and the reading of the scrolls.

Though I am of the tribe of Judah, my name is Simeon. All my life, my teachers and rabbis said I was well named. My name means *harkening*. They would call me the little listener. When I was a boy, there was a Levite who would tell us, the children, stories of our history every Sabbath day. Sometimes it seemed the scrolls were nothing but a roll book, name after name—he begat him begat her. But many days he read us stories of the great deliverers of Israel.

We learned that the Lord Almighty had chosen us, the Jews, above all nations. When we cried out to Him, He rescued us. He used men and women from all backgrounds to liberate us from our enemies. I loved those days, those stories of faith-filled heroes like Gideon and Samson, Deborah and Esther, Joshua and Elijah.

The stories stirred up a yearning deep inside me to see the Lord's hand of deliverance once again. In those days it was the Philistines, or the Babylonians, or the Assyrians. Today, Rome occupies the holy city and all of our lands.

Some say the Lord has abandoned us, that we are a godforsaken nation because of our repeated rebellions. But they forget the promise God made to our people. He would send Messiah. The scrolls speak of One who would be born not far from here, in Bethlehem, born of the root of Jesse, the tribe of Judah, the son of David. He would be a deliverer. He

15

would set us free once and for all from the hand of our oppressors. He would reign on the throne of David. The kingdom He would establish in Israel would have no end.

O how I longed to see this Messiah!

When I was a boy, I didn't understand the need. My parents protected us from the indignities and persecutions we suffered as an occupied people. As I became a man and began to raise my own family, I felt the oppression firsthand. They let us worship after a fashion, but they demanded our money, tribute to their Caesars. They required us to give our children to serve them, to do their menial tasks, all the heavy lifting. It was hardly any different than what our forefathers suffered in Egypt.

I said I was a good listener. Sometimes I heard things—heard things in my spirit. It was hard to explain. In the scrolls, we read of seers—those who had visions, even those who encountered angels. But I heard the voice of the Lord. At first I told everyone about it, but they looked at me like I needed special help, so I stopped sharing what I heard.

Initially I wasn't sure if it was the voice of the Lord, but the things I heard could always be found in the scrolls. I would write out the message I'd received and read it to the rabbi. He would open the scrolls and show me a prophecy that said the same thing. It confirmed what I had heard.

About twenty years ago now—I think I was in my sixtieth year—I heard something that has thrilled my soul for these two decades: the Holy Spirit of the Almighty told me I would see this Messiah with my own eyes before I tasted death.

This I never shared with anyone. It was one thing to compare what you heard in your meditations to what was written in the scrolls, but this was so personal. Yet, I knew what I had heard. There was no question in my mind, because I had tested that voice so many times. I knew the voice of my Lord.

It has been twenty years. There have been days when I thought I missed it and days when I thought I was crazy. But somewhere inside, I knew I would see this Long Expected One, the Lord's Anointed.

It was eight days ago that I heard it once again.

"The time is near."

I began to fast and pray. I would head to the temple every day and worship before the Lord.

Today when I awoke, the Spirit of the Lord came upon me; that's the only way I can describe it. It was not like in the past when I heard things. This was the presence of Holiness. I knew this must be the day, so I dressed and headed to the temple. I didn't break my fast.

As I stood in the temple and ministered to the Lord, a couple came in with an infant. I could see they had come to dedicate Him to the Lord. As they stepped into the court where I was worshipping, my spirit leapt for joy. This child—this infant—was the One, the Promised Messiah.

As they approached, I went to them and fell to my knees before this One born King of the Jews. The young mother handed the child to me, and I wept for joy.

I cried out:

"God, you can now release your servant; release me in peace as you promised. With my own eyes I've seen your salvation; it's now out in the open for everyone to see: A God-revealing light to the non-Jewish nations, and of glory for your people Israel."

As I looked into the eyes of my Lord, His Spirit rose up in me, and I spoke what I heard:

"This child marks both the failure and the recovery of many in Israel, A figure misunderstood and contradicted— the pain of a sword-thrust through you— But the rejection will force honesty, as God reveals who they really are."

My heart can barely contain the joy and peace I feel. I have been old, but today all things are new. Though our oppression has not changed, today I am free. Though my joints ache and my eyes aren't what they used to be, I am leaping for joy, and I have seen the Lord's salvation.

I am ready to go to the bosom of Abraham today, where I can tell my story to those who have gone before.

The day of deliverance is here.

Blessed be the name of the Lord.

~~~

To read the original story, see Luke 2:25-35.

At the very time Simeon was praying, she showed up,
broke into an anthem of praise to God,
and talked about the child to all who were waiting
expectantly for the freeing of Jerusalem.
Luke 2:38

I'VE BEEN WAITING FOR YOU

ANNA

This is the One, the promised Messiah. This babe is the one foretold. Thanks be to God. Thanks be to the Lord.

The Lord let me see this in a vision when I first began to prophesy. It was shortly after my husband died, almost sixty years ago now, and it's the reason I serve here in the temple.

The rabbi married my husband and me just down the steps in the outer courts. I was only sixteen years old; my Avram was approaching thirty. We lived in Jerusalem, not far from the sheep gate. We could not have children, but before we went to the doctor to find out why, my Avram took a fever. After only seven years of marriage, he was gone. I was alone.

We were always devout. We prayed together, and he taught me every week. At mealtime we would sit and discuss what the scriptures said. He would tell me what the men read in the temple.

When my husband died, I could no longer afford to live in my home outside the temple. I approached one of the priests and asked if there was something I could do within the gates. He allowed me to work in the outer courts. I would clean up every evening after the crowds headed to their homes or lodgings. He allowed me to live in a small room on the temple's outer wall.

At first I felt ashamed, cleaning up after all those filthy animals. Picking up the litter scattered by the merchants and their customers in the temple market humbled me. But soon I realized I could do it as an act of worship to the Lord God of Israel.

Shortly after Avram's death, I began to see. I had glimpses—flashes, at first—of things to come. I remember the first time I realized what was happening.

A woman, only days from the delivery of her child, came into the courts. She looked tired and burdened. As I watched her, she changed before me. No longer struggling to walk and bent from the weight of the child within, she was standing upright with babe in arms—a baby boy with a full head of hair. Her countenance expressed the joy in her heart. Even the color of her clothes had changed.

It was less than two months later when she walked past me with her boy, and she was wearing the dress I saw in my vision. I didn't say or do anything about it then, but it happened more and more. Some things I saw would later come to pass. Others . . . well, I don't know if I missed them or if I just didn't understand what I was seeing.

There was one vision I had over and over, and today I am standing right in the middle of it. In my vision, I saw a young woman come into the courts with an older man. She carried a newborn in her arms. It reminded me of my Avram and me. This was our dream, to bring our own child to the temple for dedication. But there was something special about this couple. In my vision I saw the old man, that Simeon fellow who seemed to start every conversation with "When Messiah comes," take the babe from the young girl. He held Him up at eye level and began to speak. I couldn't make out the words, but I saw tears in his eyes.

And it's happening, this day I have seen for sixty years. Thanks be to the Almighty One. Right here and right now Messiah is in His temple dressed for His dedication.

I timidly approached the couple.

"May I hold the child?"

The young mother put Him in my arms.

"Do you know who He is?"

It was a strange question to be asking a mother about her own child, but she wasn't surprised. She just nods and said,

"We know. His name is Jesus."

They went on to see the priest, but I have not stopped telling everyone I see that Messiah has come to His temple.

~~~

To read the original story, see Luke 2:36-38.

They entered the house and saw the child in the arms of Mary,
his mother. Overcome, they kneeled and worshiped him.
Then they opened their luggage and presented gifts:
gold, frankincense, myrrh.
Matthew 2:11

A STAR SPEAKS

MAGI

Last night I had a dream—at least I think it was a dream. An angel stood before me and told me not to trust Herod, but to leave without passing back through Jerusalem.

In days past, my nation, Babylon, took captive many people from many places. Most of the people we conquered were content to be alive and, over time, assimilated to our culture. I don't suppose anyone liked slavery or living in foreign lands. But our king in those days, Nebuchadnezzar, would have our captives evaluated. He believed it was a waste to put great minds in the fields or strong bodies in the counting house. People were not as likely to revolt if they were capable in their occupations.

You're probably wondering who I am and what I'm doing here in Bethlehem. Some call my sect stargazers; some think we're magicians. In reality, we're students—students of the wisdom we've gleaned from the cultures we have conquered.

When I finished my apprenticeship about five years back, I took on the writings from a peculiar people, the Hebrews.

The strange thing about these Jews is that they would never assimilate. They never became Babylonians—not even Babylonian captives. They were Jews and only Jews. They kept their customs and their ways. They dressed alike and stayed together. There were some, of course, who intermarried and some who left the worship of their God. Some even mixed their religions with others in our massive melting pot of culture. But most Hebrews held tight to their traditions and to their God.

One notable Hebrew captive was a young man named Belteshazzar. His Hebrew name was Daniel. I call him "the dreamer." He and a few of his fellow Jews rose to places of great influence in Nebuchadnezzar's court. He was a seer. He could read dreams and was able to see into the future. He often spoke of a coming messiah revealed in the Hebrew writings. This deliverer would come to release captive Israel. He spoke of a king for the Jews who would come when the time was right.

One night about two years ago, a new star appeared in the heavens. We called it a star, but it was unlike any we'd studied before. Most of the other stars circled the night sky, but this star was always right overhead. We observed it for a few weeks, and there it stood every clear night, shining bright and strong.

We began calculations to determine what it might be and what it might mean, and everything pointed to Israel.

We brought this information to our nation's leadership. They wanted nothing to do with a king born in the land now occupied by the Romans. Our day had past, and Rome was a force far beyond our grasp.

My fellow astronomers and I began to look to others to support a journey to see what this star meant. As we told of the ancient stories of a king born in Jerusalem and sent from the Hebrew God, many listened. There were many who still held to the religion of the Hebrews.

They donated supplies for our journey and gifts for this king—most notably gold, frankincense, and myrrh. It took a few months more to gather enough support to make the nine-hundred-mile journey. By the time we were ready to travel, we had not only accumulated much to offer this new king, but we'd gathered quite a following.

We decided to take the route used by Israel when they made the trek back to their land. 450 years ago, Ezra led many Hebrews back to Jerusalem to rebuild the city and their temple. Rather than heading straight across the desert toward the star, we traveled northeast along the Euphrates and then south along the Jordan River.

We arrived in Jerusalem three days ago and met with Herod and his counselors. They directed us to Bethlehem. He offered us a handsome reward if we returned and guided him to this young king. I see now that he was plotting to destroy the child and this threat to his own reign.

Yesterday, after almost two years of planning and travel, we met with this child king. I was beginning to fear that the whole thing was a huge mistake, but nothing could have been further from the truth.

It was late afternoon by the time we reached Bethlehem. We asked around, yet no one knew of a boy king. We stopped and considered the star once more as evening approached. It seemed to be guiding us. I can't explain how we knew, but we followed this guide right to the house where Jesus was staying.

We knocked on the door. The man who greeted us seemed unsure what to make of our foreign garb and the entourage that followed after us. I was not sure what to say either. My heart raced.

"Is this the home of the King?" I asked, unable to contain my excitement.

When I said it, I saw the tension leave his face.

"You must mean the child, Jesus. Wait here," he replied.

I could see that the home was far too small to welcome our company, so we waited without while the man of the house left us. Moments later, he returned with a couple and their young child.

"This is Joseph of Nazareth and his wife, Mary, and her child, Jesus."

Mary's eyes grew when she saw our troupe, and she drew Jesus behind Joseph.

"What business do you have with us?" Joseph said.

I then fell to one knee as I looked upon the child. He looked like any other Hebrew boy, but there was something different in the air. I sensed a calm flowing out of the house. The curious boy peeked around Joseph's legs and stared at us, his little head cocked. I'm sure we looked strange to these Jews, with our camels and colorful robes.

"We have come to pay homage to the One born King of the Jews. Is this the child? Is this the One the prophets foretold, the One called Emanuel?" I said.

"Yes," Mary said. "His name is Jesus, and His miraculous birth was foretold by our prophets for hundreds of years."

"We have come to worship this Messiah of the Jews with gifts from our nation."

Then we presented our many gifts. The gold we carried made a fitting offering for a king and the frankincense a worthy homage to a holy man. The myrrh was a curiosity to me, because it was so melancholy. Yes, it was a precious and costly gift, but it spoke of death, which did not seem a fitting gift for child or king.

Our gifts accepted, the young couple took us into town to find a place for our party to stay the night. The inn was full but offered to let us rest in their stable. Before they left us for the night, Mary told me this was the place of the child's birth.

How could it be that One so important, foreseen for centuries, could be born in such lowly surroundings and to such common people? Their house was tiny, and there were no attendants or servants to care for Him. This child of peace and grace should be in Jerusalem, in the great palace there.

It was as I slept in the hay that I had the dream. A man—an angel perhaps—stood before me and warned me not to return to Herod, but to go home another way. We returned to the house the next morning and told the couple of my dream. Some wanted to stay in Bethlehem and serve the young king, but his parents insisted we go, for our safety and theirs.

There is something within me that does not want to leave. This place has a hold on me. The child has captured my imagination. I don't want to leave, but how can I stay?

What will become of this young king?

~~~

To read the original story, see Matthew 2:1-12.

MINISTRY

"We've found the One Moses wrote of in the Law,
the One preached by the prophets.
It's Jesus, Joseph's son, the one from Nazareth!"
John 1:45-46

UNDER THE FIG TREE

NATHANAEL

"Do you have to say everything that comes into that tiny brain, Nate?"

I'm not sure I can tell you how many times I heard that. Mom, Dad, my brother Philip, especially—they're all tired of my incessant response: "But it's the truth!"

I always had to be right. The youngest child of five, I felt my words carried no weight with the others. As a child, more times than I would like to admit, I was in trouble for talking back to the rabbi or a friend's parent. I even corrected a priest once, and boy was I in trouble then! My response? "But it's the truth!"

Philip and I were close in age and did everything together, and we always contradicted each other. When we were kids, it was because we got frustrated with each other. Now I suppose it's just habit. It's a sort of love language, you might say.

Yet today truth betrayed me. It nearly cost me everything. I came right up to a crossroad and almost turned away from Truth. Deep Truth.

I had a sense of expectation as I pondered the scriptures before dawn this morning. It was too warm to sleep, so I sat beneath the fig tree and mulled over the words of the prophet Isaiah.

As I sat there in the predawn warmth, I let my mind work through the questions that came unbidden. Isaiah spoke of a Man of sorrows. Who was this One crushed for our iniquities, poured out to death, bearing the sins of many? Who was this lamb, silent before His accusers? Would Messiah ever come?

Little did I know that I would meet Him that day. If my demand for "truth" didn't keep me from considering the man from Galilee, I would take up my cross and follow this lamb Isaiah foretold.

"Nate? Nate! Wake up!"

I opened my eyes to see Philip, breathless and giddy, standing over me. I guess I'd drifted off.

"We've found Messiah, the Nazarene. Jesus!"

Philip's words seemed like a bad joke. Nazareth? Not Bethlehem? Can't be. I was ready to dismiss the whole matter. He knew as well as I did that Messiah was to be born in Bethlehem of Judea, not up north in Galilee. Those northern folk are almost as watered down as the Samaritans.

"What possible good can come out of that compromised, worthless city?" I asked.

"Come and see!" And he was off, running.

I stood at a crossroad, yet I was still unaware of how important those next few moments would be. Philip and I argued all the time, but he's no fool. He wouldn't follow some obvious imposter. We've both seen others who claimed to be messiah. We'd unraveled their savior claims one by one and come to the truth.

So how could Philip fall for this obvious pretender?

I followed without conviction.

As I approached, this Nazarene spoke the words that would alter my path forever:

"...*before Philip called you here, I saw you under the fig tree.*"

As I pondered Isaiah's lamb, I allowed my heart to desire the coming of this Messiah. This Nazarene was watching? Surely this was the Messiah.

What could I do but follow Him? I followed Philip and found the Messiah, the One whose heart I touched as I searched the scriptures.

Today I take up the cross—His cross—and follow this lamb.

~~~

To read the original story, see John 1:45-51.

When the sun went down,
everyone who had anyone sick with some ailment
or other brought them to him.
One by one he placed his hands on them and healed them.
Luke 4:40

HEALER

BLIND MAN

I heard the door open, and my wife told me it was Him, the young carpenter, looking out at a sea of broken people. What would He say? Would He send us back to our homes? When we left the house, I had no idea the whole town would be there. He turned to the fisherman and said something about His Father's business. Then he headed down the steps and into the throng.

I should start at the beginning.

The day began, like most Sabbaths, with my family in the synagogue. My wife, Rebecca, walked me through town to our little gathering place every Sabbath day. She left me with the men and went over to stand with the women. She has been my guide for fifteen long years, ever since the kiln in my shop exploded and left me without sight, so the men allowed her to bring me to my seat.

Today, that young man, Jesus, read from the scrolls. He opened to the place where the prophet Isaiah spoke of our coming Messiah:

"God's Spirit is on me; He's chosen me to preach the Message of good news to the poor, Sent me to announce pardon to prisoners and recovery of sight to the blind, To set the burdened and battered free, to announce, 'This is God's year to act!'"

The rabbi rose to take the scroll back from Him and make his remarks, but he never got the chance. As the young man closed the scroll, He looked up and with an air of authority declared:

"You've just heard Scripture make history. It came true just now in this place."

The rabbi had no idea what to do. The carpenter's son had never done anything like that before. To be honest, no one but the rabbi had ever spoken about the scriptures to us in the meeting. We were a small congregation, all of us working men.

The way He spoke struck me. The rabbi always told us what the learned men thought the passages might mean. He quoted this scholar and that prophet. He compared the possibilities. No man had ever stood and spoken with such conviction.

As we disbursed and my wife hurried me back to the house for dinner, I heard the men talking. As we moved through the streets, pockets of people buzzed with the story of what happened in the synagogue.

When I mentioned His reading the part where Isaiah spoke of blind eyes opened, Rebecca said we must find Him. I tried to explain to her that it was a metaphor and that Isaiah spoke not of the physical eyes but the spiritual. I tried to convince her that my eyes were not closed by disease or an act of God but by an accident, and that was different. My eyes were forfeited due to my own carelessness. It was my fault.

But she insisted that when the sun set we should find Him. She'd heard talk of Him staying over at the fisherman's house.

As the sun went down and the Sabbath ended, she got me my cloak and took my arm. It was impossible to stop my Rebecca when she got an idea in her head.

The streets teemed with people, which was strange for the evening of the first day. It had the feel of a feast day, when we would all go together to the house of the Lord, but this time the flow moved toward the fisherman's home.

When we arrived, Rebecca told me there were dozens of people there. Some were on mats, some on litters, and some just lay on the dusty road. Others like me came with guides standing in the gaps.

That's when I heard the door open. I could hear the murmur of His voice as He moved through the crowd. Suddenly there was an outburst. Someone was yelling. At first I thought it had all gone wrong; perhaps someone had been trampled. Rebecca screamed and then began to laugh. She told me it was Micah from a few doors down. He was on his feet! An oxcart had crippled my neighbor when it tumbled over on him three years back.

Again there was muttering I could not make out and another shout. Then I heard a voice I had not heard in a decade. It was an old friend from my childhood who had not been . . . well, how do I say it? He just had not been right for years. His family had to restrain him and keep him in the house. Now he was calling out praises and thanksgiving to the Almighty.

Then I felt a hand on my shoulder, and I heard His voice. He asked me why I was there. Rebecca started to speak for me, but He stilled her and raised my chin. With one eye missing and the other useless, my downcast posture had become part of me. I didn't want to frighten anyone.

He asked me again, and He used my name. "Eli, what do you want from Me?"

My head was spinning. Should I explain about the accident? Should I tell Him I am getting along fine without my eyes? What do I say to this man?

I finally said, "Can you open my eye?"

I think He chuckled.

Then He touched me, but it was my empty eye socket upon which His fingers rested. Immediately, the whole side of my face was on fire. Then, like a foot that had fallen asleep, it started to tingle. I felt pressure on my brow as a new eye formed in the empty socket. The sensation was so stunning that I didn't even realize I was beginning to sense light with the other eye.

The first thing I did with my new eye was cry. My joy and astonishment were overwhelming. I fell to my knees and thanked Him, but He simply moved on to the next person.

I sat there on the side of the road and watched as He went from person to person, taking time to speak to everyone. As He did, wholeness pervaded each soul He touched. The sun had been down for a few hours by the time we headed back to our home.

All my years we have prayed Elijah would come, that the Almighty would send a deliverer, a Messiah. Today He is here, and He touched me.

~~~

To read the original story, see Luke 4:18-41.

"Come see a man who knew all about the things I did,
who knows me inside and out.
Do you think this could be the Messiah?"
John 4:29

What I Found at the Well

Samaritan Woman

I wasn't always this way: a pariah, an outcast from society, cut off from my children, forgotten by those I once loved. Now, I live day to day. Then, I had a future. Hopes. Dreams.

When I was a young girl, I dreamed of the day when I would be the one in the white dress. I would be the one swept away by the dashing and gentle man. I would be the one celebrated, congratulated. The young girls would sing and dance around me.

I remember when my fortunes began to turn. As a woman in a man's world, it wasn't like I had much to say in the matter. My first husband threw me out one day. I know it wasn't the first time I didn't have a meal ready for him when he came in, but was that all I was to him? A cook?

He was nearly three times my age. When we married, his forty-six years could have been a hundred to me. He was a butcher, and my father made the match thinking I would not go hungry. At sixteen, I had done some cooking, but our family was large, and I was the youngest girl. I never learned how to manage a kitchen or plan a meal.

The marriage lasted less than two years. Now instead of a silly sixteen-year-old girl, I was a divorced woman with a broken heart at seventeen. He and his new wife kept my baby, my only joy for the last eight months.

My parents let me back in my childhood home, but things were not the same. They looked at me with different eyes. Rather than seeing my pain, they saw the shame I brought them.

My father tried for a couple years to find me a match, but a good man did not want a divorced woman.

That's when I began to settle. I settled four more times, and each time I found myself back on the street. Now I live with a man, and he's a brute. He does not have any interest in marrying me; he just wants someone to boss around. I have finally learned to get supper on the table promptly, since the alternative is so painful.

After my second marriage, the women in Sychar began to talk. It got worse and worse, until I just didn't want to be seen in town anymore. Every time I showed up in the village, my shame burned me. It was like holding my hand over an open flame. When I entered a shop or market, all the talking stopped and the glaring began.

Twice a day—morning and evening—since the day I was first married, it fell to me to fetch the water. A few years back, I stopped going with the rest of the women. As their distaste for me grew, I looked for different times and other places to find water. I began to travel all the way out to Jacob's well. It was deeper than the one in town, so I needed to bring more rope. It was fifteen minutes farther away, but it was private in the heat of the day.

When I got to the well today, I was a bit surprised to find a man there. Not just a man, but a Jew. I could tell by the locks of hair curling down beside his cheeks and by his Galilean accent. I can't even imagine how he came to be there.

It was rare to see a Jew in Samaria. They didn't like us. They didn't like our animals. They didn't like our roads. They didn't like anything about us.

This Jew looked tired, having most likely spent hours traveling, and he had nothing with him—no waterskins, no luggage, no food. Who traveled across this desolate tract without water? But here he was.

I was hesitant to approach. The Jews could get pretty hostile toward Samaritans. The fighting wasn't of a physical nature, but there was no love lost in our dealings.

Then, out of the blue, He spoke to me.

"Will you give me a drink?"

I looked up. I had not let my eyes meet His. Eye contact was usually painful for me; the scorn or condemnation I found in most eyes drove mine to the ground. But when He spoke it startled me, put me off-balance.

At first I thought I would just ignore Him. This Jew could only have malice in mind. But I could feel His eyes on me. He did not turn away and was not put off by my silence. He just sat there on the edge of the well and watched me. When I finally looked up and met His gaze, something in His eyes said He was there just for me. He didn't look at me like other men. He was looking at the "little-girl me"—like my father used to when I sat on his lap. There was somehow safety in His gaze.

Still, this could not end well for me, so I took another moment, gathered my wits, and put up my guard.

"You're a Jew and I'm a Samaritan, a woman. How can you ask me for a drink?"

Then He started talking to me about some living water. At first I didn't get it. I couldn't tell if He was flirting with me or making fun of me. But there was something in His tone, in His way, something completely genuine.

Next thing I knew, He told me to call for my husband.

There it was again. Every time I dared to hope for something good, for a new relationship, my past stood like a locked gate before me, an iron barrier between me and life.

I wanted the living water. I wanted eternal life. But who would ever love someone with my past?

"I'm not married," I mumbled. It was true after a fashion. The man of my house won't even let my children visit when he's at home. He would never marry me—love me.

He waited a beat. My heart waited, too. Did He know I was bending the truth?

"That's nicely put: 'I have no husband.' You've had five husbands, and the man you're living with now isn't even your husband. You spoke the truth there, sure enough."

How could He know these things? They say Messiah will come, and when He comes He will tell us all things. Could this be Him?

We spoke of other things—of temples and worship, of Mount Gerizim and Jerusalem. But what I wanted to ask Him—Are you the One?—I couldn't get my tongue to say the words.

Finally I edged up on the question.

"I do know that the Messiah is coming. When he arrives, we'll get the whole story."

His answer broke the iron gate, and the floods began to flow. His answer was like living water to my soul.

"I AM He."

This Man-Jew-Prophet-Messiah-Savior of the World, this Jesus, flooded my soul with living water. He made me a temple, a place of worship to the One True God. And He did it knowing who I was and what I'd done. He knew me—all of me—and loved me.

Today, when I lie down to sleep, it's not in blankets of shame. The flood within me springs up to life daily.

The acceptance I pined for these forty years, I found at the well.

The cleansing I wept for year after year, I found at the well.

Come! See a man who told me everything I ever did. Could this be the Messiah?

~~~

To read the original story, see John 4:1-29.

Just give the order and my servant will get well.
Luke 7:7

Soldiers, Slaves, and Friends

Centurion

I am a man under authority, charged with the care and management of one hundred Roman soldiers. Believe me, it is no small task. There is never a dull moment. Just keeping the peace among such a band is a full-time job. Take dozens of men away from their families and feed them military rations for months at a time, and it can get a bit edgy.

But one thing I will say about Roman soldiers—when I bark, they obey. If I tell them to rally, they are ready to march in minutes. I lead, they follow; I send them, they go. They are a disciplined lot, which speaks volumes about the training program for Rome's army.

As a man under authority myself, I understand why. My group of one hundred soldiers is only a small part of the legion tasked with keeping peace here in Galilee. There are 5,600 Roman soldiers spread throughout the region and another fifty-eight centurions. We all answer up the line. When we get commands from Rome, believe me, we act.

I could never manage all I am responsible for without my manservant, though. He keeps it all together for me. I never have to think about the mundane stuff of life. He always makes sure I have the right uniform and equipment ready to go. It seems like he can read my mind sometimes. He is always looking for ways to anticipate my needs and make my life easier. What would I do without him?

I have spent a decade serving here in this Jewish community. The Hebrews have impressed me time and time again with their value for culture and tradition. We—Rome--have come into their lands and taken control of their government. Rome brings its own culture when we occupy a land. The plan is assimilation, but these Jews persist with their worship of this God called Yahweh. I never heard one say His name aloud. They say man's mouth is too profane to bear such a holy name.

I have come to love the people and their ways. Our normal model is to turn our foreign conquests into "little Romes," changing their cultures, but we have not been able to change these Jews. I figured, why fight it? I had a synagogue built for them. They have been so appreciative. I have become good friends with many of them. Some even invite me to family celebrations.

Last month, I noticed a look on my manservant's face, sort of a grimace. I asked him what was up, and he said he was feeling some pain, but he told me I shouldn't worry about him. The pain worsened for a couple weeks, until he was no longer able to work.

Now he is bedridden, paralyzed, and I am afraid he is going to die. He is in constant pain. The doctors—and I have called in many—poke and prod, but to no avail.

My good friend, Mordcha, has been telling me of a Jewish teacher who is moving from town to town around the area. This man, Jesus, has been healing everyone who comes to Him. Mordcha tells me there are hundreds of folks following Him everywhere He goes.

But I am not a Jew. Why would He step foot in my house?

And yet, this man clearly had authority over these killing diseases. With that kind of authority, He would not even have to come. He could just give the command, speak the word, and this healing power He wields would carry out His orders. I don't get how He does it, but I understand what it is to give and take commands.

I hear Jesus is somewhere near Capernaum, which is only an hour's ride from here. I will lend Mordcha my horse, and ask him to ask Jesus to command this disease out of my servant.

Just realizing there is hope, I feel better today. When I first bought this manservant, I basically thought of him as property. But today I depend on him, and we have become friends. I hate the thought of losing him.

Wait! What's that sound? It's him, my servant, up and around and out of bed. And it has not even been two hours since my friend left! My man is standing before me pain free, his strength returned.

Thank God, and thanks be to this Jesus, the One who sends the Word and heals.

~~~

To read the original story, see Luke 7:2-10.

"Young man, I tell you: Get up."
Luke 7:15

ALIVE

WIDOW OF NAIN

ALIVE! My son is alive, and I have the prophet, Jesus, to thank for it.

I thought I had finally lost everything, but today He gave me a fresh start.

After Amit, my husband, died, I felt empty and broken, like half a woman. Once he was gone, I could no longer keep the home we had made. I took Kfir, my son, and went to live with my parents.

When my Amit passed on, I lost a husband, a house, and his covering. But most of all, I lost my friend. His very name meant *friend*. It was perfect. Before he was anything else to me, he was my friend. We grew up together, and we planned to grow old together. But it was not to be.

Kfir was not yet thirteen when we lost his father, not quite a man. At first he tried to step up and be the man of the house, but it wore on my little lion cub and, as time went on, resentment grew. He resented his father for leaving him. He resented me for taking him back to his grandparents' house. He resented them for putting him in a room with an aunt who was his junior. Moreover, he resented the Lord for putting him into such an ugly life.

The same months and years that healed my hurts and dimmed the loss I felt seemed to make his anguish grow. With each passing birthday, he grew more and more distant, until it seemed I had lost him, too. It was just after his sixteenth birthday when he left the house and left the synagogue. I saw him from time to time, but he would not make eye contact.

Then about a month ago, he got sick. He told me he was only uncomfortable after he ate. He said he thought it would pass, but it got worse and worse, until he couldn't keep his food down. That's when he came back home.

I remember thinking, "Thank you, Lord, for bringing my boy home." But after the first long night, I knew this was not the Lord's doing. I saw in his eyes a cry for help. Yes, I had my Kfir, my little lion cub, in my arms once again, but he was dying. Doctors came and went, each with a different idea for helping my boy to hold some food, but it was not to be.

I even called our rabbi, and he brought a priest to the house. When they heard my story, they wouldn't pray for him. They said this torture, this torment my son faced, was the judgment of the Lord and to make an offering would be an abomination. They told me the Almighty would not hear the prayers of the rebellious.

Two days ago, death took my son while he lay in my arms. When he left me, he left me alone.

Our law requires you bury your dead quickly, laying another brick on my heavy heart. I just wanted to hold him in my arms. I just wanted one last look in his eyes. My father helped me get him a coffin and dress him. He even gathered my brothers to carry him to the place we would bury him—a place I knew all too well. The place my Amit lay buried these three years.

As we moved into our little town of Nain, we found the road completely blocked, hundreds of people in every direction. They strained and pressed in to hear as the man in the center of it all was talking—teaching, I think. My brothers eked their way through the middle of the street, Kfir's coffin held high.

My heart cried out to the Lord, "Why is this so hard? I just want to bury my son!" I broke down and wept in earnest. The weight of it all—the loss of my husband, the abandonment and then death of my boy, the rejection of the leaders—it all gushed out in a torrent of tears.

I bumped into my dear boy's box when we came to an abrupt halt. It disoriented me a bit. Then I heard the voice that had been teaching moments earlier say:

"Don't cry."

I'm not sure what stopped my tears. It may have been fury, or indignation, or shock, or just confusion. I wiped my eyes, trying to find the words that would rescue me from this crowd. I wanted to get on with—get through—this most horrible of days.

Then our eyes met. He felt my pain; I could see it in His eyes. He was not trying to placate me, or control me, or hush me. He knew what I felt.

He knew the hurt. He knew the shame. He knew the guilt. I don't know how this man could understand the heart of a woman, a widow, a mother with no children. I don't know.

He put His hand on the rough-hewn coffin and spoke to my son.

"Young man, I tell you: Get up."

The last was more of a shout; it had the feel of a command, like my Amit used to stop Kfir when he was in danger.

It was our tradition to keep the coffin open for the procession. People could have one last look at the dead before we surrendered them to the ground. I was so glad we did, because as His words echoed through the streets, Kfir began to stir.

First it was just . . . I don't know . . . like a flutter. But then all at once, he gulped in a mouthful of air and spoke! When he started speaking, I didn't know what he was saying, but then I understood. It was not normal street talk; it was the formal Hebrew of the temple. He was reciting the portion of Torah he'd memorized and recited at his bar mitzvah.

His eyes opened and he sat up. Then he understood what was going on, and he wept. As they lowered the coffin, he climbed out and came to me. His embrace engulfed me and our tears mingled. Then we turned and embraced Him, Jesus, this One sent from God.

Was He just a prophet? A messenger? An angel? Who was this Jesus? As we embraced Him, the magnitude of what had occurred suddenly hit us. We were overcome with fear, awe, and wonder. We let go of Him and fell to our knees. As we did, we noticed everyone in the street had bowed low.

Murmurs rippled around us. What kind of prophet was this? Had the Lord come in a man's body? No other man had done such things among us. Surely this was the Son of God.

Those same questions floated around my mind, and I had no answer. But I know this: Today I received my son from the dead. We will follow this Nazarene.

~~~

To read the original story, see Luke 7:11-16.

"Wind and sea at his beck and call!"
Mark 4:41

HUSH

MATTHEW

The strangest thing happened yesterday. I have to tell you this story. I would never have believed it if I had not been right there on the boat. Every day with Jesus is just amazing, but today . . . I'm not even sure I can make you believe this. I'm still running through it in my head. Thomas and Andrew and I compared notes all the way back from the docks tonight.

It all started this morning as we left the synagogue. Right in the middle of the crowd, a leper walked up, and Jesus healed him on the spot. Then a Roman soldier stopped us and talked with the Master about his servant. When we got to Peter and Andrew's house, Jesus healed Peter's mother-in-law. She'd had a fever for months, and just like that, she was back to serving us Sabbath dinner.

We spent a few blessed hours around the table, laughing and talking and always learning. Somehow, Jesus managed to teach us about the kingdom of Heaven even when He was just playing around with us.

As we left the house, we found a multitude of people pressing in at the door. The sick and infirm covered every inch of yard and street. There were beds and stretchers and people lying in the dust. Here and there were men and women who looked possessed.

Mind you, it was already after sunset, but Jesus went to each one. He asked what they needed, and He ministered, touched, loved, and cared for every single one of them. He spoke their names. He touched their wounds. He held their hands. He rebuked the demons. He didn't leave until every single person was whole.

What an amazing day it was! Right? But there was more to come! I thought we would spend the night at Peter's house, but Jesus headed

40

down to the docks. He climbed right on Zebedee's boat—the one James and John brought up a few days ago.

Jesus asked John to head for the other side of the lake, and then He went to the stern and lay down on the cushioned bench across the back. He was asleep in minutes.

Suddenly, the wind picked up, as it often did on the Sea of Galilee. Before I knew it, the waves went crazy, crashing over the sides of the boat. The water rose to my knees in minutes. Peter, Andrew, James, and John ran bow to stern, port and starboard, yelling words I didn't understand. After all, they practically lived on boats.

They told me to grab this, haul that, crank the other thing. I'm a tax collector! What do I know? They shouted to me to wake Jesus before He drowned.

We all screamed to Jesus, while two of the boys tried to ready the lifeboats. The sea opened wide, threatening to swallow us whole. I thought we were going to die.

Finally Jesus awoke and dropped His feet down into the water on the deck. He stretched as He rose slowly to His feet, like He wasn't quite awake yet. We continued to shout:

"Master, save us! We're going down!"

"Teacher, is it nothing to you that we're going down?"

"Master, Master, we're going to drown!"

At that moment, the most astonishing thing happened. He looked over the port side of the boat, just noticing the storm crashing around us.

"Hush! Quiet down," He said.

In an instant, the sea was as flat as glass. It was as though the smallest ripple would shatter the perfect reflection of holiness that surrounded us on every side.

He turned to us, and I could not read the look on His face. Was He angry? Amused? Was He just exasperated with us? Honestly, I'm still not sure. I was in shock.

"Why were you afraid?" He asked. Then I looked down and noticed the deck was dry. "Where is your faith?"

I looked over at Thomas, and I think we said in, unison, "Who is this? What kind of person can talk to the wind and the sea and they obey?"

I'm still trying to figure out what He meant. He asked us where our faith was. He wanted us to see that waking Him shouldn't have been necessary; we should have been able to deal with the storm ourselves.

He was so calm. I think He actually went back and finished His nap, but I'm not sure I will ever be able to sleep again. With three simple words, the peace that let this man sleep in a storm silenced the wind and the waves.

What manner of man is this?

~~~

To read the original story, see Matthew 8:1-27, Mark 4:35-41, and Luke 8:22-25.

"Son, I forgive your sins."
Mark 2:5

ARISE, TAKE UP YOUR BED AND WALK

BOYHOOD FRIEND OF JESUS

My friend, Abram, said He was back in town. That upstart, Jesus. Such a know-it-all. For the last two decades, we've rubbed shoulders. We learned Hebrew together, studied the scriptures together.

I always loved school and learning. My father wanted me to become a rabbi, so he let me stay in school when most of the others went back to their family businesses.

And until a few months ago, that's how it was with Jesus. He was just a working man, running the business His father left him. He was a carpenter. In fact, He made my writing desk and this chair.

When we were in school together, He always challenged the rabbis. He was not disrespectful, but He asked such amazing, profound questions. I liked him, for the most part, but He rarely joined in with us outside of school. He was always in His house or in the workshop— reading, studying, or praying. He pursued His studies with a singular focus. I guess you could call Him a bookworm. If there was something to know about the Almighty, Jesus wanted to know.

Jesus and His new band of—I don't know what to call them. Students?—arrived late last night by boat from the other side of the lake, and they were a mess. It looked as though they hadn't slept in days, perhaps not since they left the night of the freak storm on the lake.

Sometime in the middle of the morning, I looked out the window and noticed a group gathered near Joseph's shop. As my family lived just across the way, I wandered over to see what was going on.

Jesus was teaching—something about the use of our time and money. The crowd kept growing and packed into Joseph's little house until you couldn't get in or out the doors. The courtyard was full, too, and the crowd backed right into the carpentry shop.

I was impressed as I looked around at the crowd. Many of the best and brightest of Galilee were gathered there. I recognized a couple Pharisees from the synagogue over in Nazareth. I heard there were even a few big shots from Jerusalem right there in our little town.

I'm not sure what it was, but there was something in the air. I felt a presence, a power I could almost reach out and touch. I had a strong feeling if I just sucked in a deep breath, the coughing fits I got in the evening would go away forever.

Suddenly, I felt something fall on my head. As I pressed back into the people behind me, a stream of dust and dirt flowed down from overhead. There was some serious clatter coming from the roof above us.

I watched as a hole opened in the roof above me—and not just a little hole. There was a crowd on the roof. By the time the commotion was over, they must have removed dozens of roof tiles. What a mess!

Four men stood on opposing corners of the gap they had created. They began to lower a stretcher, a hammock-like contraption they'd rigged with some ropes. Then it dawned on me: I knew this man, the one on the stretcher. He was the beggar who sat near the fruit stand at the market every day. I remember my father giving alms to him every time we went to the market when I was a child.

Let me tell you, the room was silent. All I heard was the trickle of debris still filtering down through the breach.

"Go ahead, ask Him!" one of the men on the roof called down to his friend.

But before the man on the stretcher could say a word, Jesus said to him:

"Son, I forgive your sins."

That's when things got confusing. Everyone started to talk at once. At least two of the Pharisees and the local rabbi tore their robes and looked for a way to get out of there, but it was just too crowded to move. I'd say this: Jesus lost His place in the synagogue today. They were crossing His name out of the book in their heads even as they struggled to find a way out of the crowd. His declaration was nothing short of blasphemy.

Jesus looked around at this new commotion. I could not make out the expression on His face. Then, His voice somehow resonating above the din, He said:

"Why are you so skeptical? Which is simpler: to say to the paraplegic, 'I forgive your sins,' or say, 'Get up take your stretcher, and start walking'?"

I'd heard stories about Jesus healing people, and I was never sure what to think. I guess I figured it was all the power of positive thinking or maybe some kind of trickery, but this boasting about forgiving sins? What sort of game was He playing?

He continued:

"Well, just so it's clear that I'm the Son of Man and authorized to do either, or both . . ."

Here He directed His attention to the man on the stretcher:

"Get up. Pick up your stretcher and go home."

Then, the man I'd seen sitting by the side of the fruit market since I was a boy bounded out of the hammock. He gathered it in his arms, pulling the ropes down from the gaping hole above him, and wound his way through the crowd and out to the street. It was no trick. I knew this man. In twenty-five years I had never seen him take a step.

I can't find words to describe my amazement. I had never heard of such authority given to a man. He never even touched the broken beggar. Jesus, who I have known all my life . . . it is as though He has the hand of the Almighty in His own. It would not surprise me if He could forgive sins.

I am packing my things tonight, and I am going to see if I can go along with Him. I want to see more. I am beginning to wonder if He could be the One, the Messiah foretold in the scriptures.

~~~

To read the original story, see Matthew 9:1-8, Mark 2:1-12, and Luke 5:17-26.

*"If I can put a finger on his robe,
I can get well."*
Mark 5:28

BLOOD IN THE SHEETS

WOMAN WITH THE ISSUE OF BLOOD

At first I thought it was my time of month.

Blood in my sheets.

I am so tired of blood in my sheets, but now I am too weak to even care.

My little one was only three then; now she is a young woman, and she is probably finding her own blood in the sheets. It's strange to think of my daughter in that way, but to me it is always blood.

I have not been able to live with her in over a decade. She and my husband live in town, in our little home right down from the market. Oh how I miss the market!

I was selling my olives there when I first noticed the twinge of pain I now know is my hemorrhage. It was the first night of thousands strung together to make up who I am, who I have become.

I was Gilda the olive girl. I sold olives in the market. I was beautiful. People always remarked about the color of my eyes. They said my eyes matched my olives.

I can't remember the last time anyone even looked at my eyes.

Now I am forgotten.

This blood—this hemorrhage—has robbed me. It's as though a thief broke in and took everything.

Not my silver, and linen, and fine china, though those are all gone, too. We sold it all to raise money for the doctors. The doctors couldn't do a thing. I went to doctors in six villages. I even went down to the hospital in Capernaum, but I returned much as I'd left, only bruised and penniless.

The thief I speak of did not walk away with my possessions; he stole my family, my dignity, my humanity, my identity. I was Gilda the olive girl. Now I am no one. I am invisible. I am a scar on the roadside, to be stepped around, avoided. Who am I? I don't have an answer.

Not long ago, some lepers were talking about a man. This man, I overheard, was wandering all over the region of Galilee, doing things I've never heard of before except at the storyteller's. Jesus, they call Him. He was opening the eyes of the blind, healing all manner of sickness, and even cleansing some lepers.

Oh that name! Jesus! The LORD is salvation. O how I need a Savior!

When I heard the stories, I felt something deep in my chest, something I had not known for ages. I felt hope. After twelve years of blood on the sheets, after a decade alone, an outcast, forgotten, I felt hope.

My first thought was to go to Him. I must have Him put His hands on me and command this blood to stop. But my own husband was unwilling to touch me. The last time he came and held my hand, they would not let him back in the congregation for a week.

The stories kept coming. He healed everyone in town, laid hands on the sick folk there. I even heard He forgave a man's sins just a few days back.

Who is this Jesus?

I began to wonder if I could get to Him through the crowds that are always thronging Him. I wondered if I could get close enough to touch Him. I remembered a story from my childhood of the day they threw a dead soldier on the corpse of an old prophet, and the soldier came back to life.

If this Jesus is anything like the old Elisha, I bet just touching the hem of His cloak would be enough to stop my bleeding. As soon as this thought entered my mind, I felt warm all over, like the healing had already started, like the LORD Himself was telling me to do it.

I knew what I had to do. He was walking by, and the crowd, as always, spread around Him like a river flowing through the street. So I went for it. I wrapped my tattered robes around me, covering as much of myself as I could. I kept my eyes to the ground and edged my way into the mob.

I could not see Him yet, but I knew He was only a few paces ahead of me. I kept saying to myself the words I'd heard deep inside my soul: "Touch the hem of His cloak. Touch the hem of His cloak." It was all I could think, all I could hear.

Then I heard a voice right in front of me.

"Master, where did Jairus say he lived? Do you think it is much farther?"

"Patience, Peter."

That voice! The heat in my body doubled, and I knew it must be Him. I dove to the ground, my outstretched hand barely brushing the fringe of His robe.

Everything stopped. I could hear my heart pounding in my chest.

The Master stopped. The crowd stopped. My heart stopped.

To my horror, Jesus turned around and said:

"Who touched me?"

Peter laughed. "Who touched You? Everyone touched You. Maybe You should ask who didn't touch You."

"Someone touched me. I felt power discharging from me."

I knew I was caught. I knew He was talking about me. I had broken the law. I had come into the crowd, making them all unclean like me. I had touched Him, and not only was I not allowed to touch anyone, but to touch this man who was not my husband . . . They could arrest me, or excommunicate me, or even stone me.

I was already on the ground, so I found my way to my knees, buried my face in my hands, and blurted out the whole thing. I waited for His verdict. What would He do? What would He say?

Then there was that voice again.

"Daughter, you took a risk of faith, and now you're healed and whole. Live well, live blessed! Be healed of your plague."

Then I understood. The heat I was feeling was right at the source of the bleeding. As the heat faded, the trickling of blood I'd felt for twelve years was gone. I knew right then and there my nightmare was over.

That was yesterday.

Today I awoke on my cot, and there was no blood.

Today I will return to my home, my husband, my beautiful daughter.

Today I will return to my life, my identity.

When Jesus healed me, He didn't just stop my bleeding. He restored everything the thief had taken.

What manner of man is this?

~~~

To read the original story, see Matthew 9:18-26, Mark 5:21-43, and Luke 8:40-56.

"Go home to your own people.
Tell them your story—what the Master did,
how he had mercy on you."
Mark 5:19

COME OUT OF THE MAN

DEMONIAC OF THE GADARENES

"Out! Get out of the man!"

The voice rumbles from across the lake like distant thunder.

It has been years since I heard anything so clearly. The rest is just a fog. Voices

So many voices.

Never quiet.

I can't remember silence.

But today there is peace.

"Get out of the man!"

Then the voices stop.

"What business do you have, Jesus, Son of the High God, messing with me? I swear to God, don't give me a hard time!"

I hear those words and realize it is my mouth crying out. I have listened to the voices for years. I hate them. This voice is one of the ringleaders, head troublemaker.

"I beg you in the name of the LORD not to torment me before my time."

This voice has never asked permission before—not in the decade he has been with me, in me. How filthy it seems to hear such a holy name in the mouth of my jailer. I realize my tormentor is afraid. Fear has been my companion for days without number, but today the fear in the air is not mine, nor that of those around me.

Do you know the worst part? Everyone is afraid of me. My children, my wife . . . even my own mother fills with terror when I'm around.

They sent me out to this valley of death. This army inside me loves it out here. They thrive on the sadness and hopelessness of this graveyard.

The town fathers have me bound, chained, but to no purpose. The mob in my body cares nothing for the flesh of my wrists and has no qualms about tearing skin and flesh to break me out of these chains.

And it's not all they tear off me. Every time I find some rags of clothing to cover myself, they tear it to shreds. My shame brings them some sick pleasure. They mark my body, bruises and cuts from the stones that litter this place. Then they expose me, naked, covered in filth and stinking like a corpse. When I want to weep they mock and laugh. When I want to pray and ask God for help and forgiveness for the wickedness inside me, they use my mouth to curse. What comes out of my mouth is even viler than my stench.

Sometimes I try to join those more fortunate than me, the dead that surround me, by cutting myself. They let me bleed, but they won't let me die.

I hate my life!

There's the voice again. "Get out of the man, you unclean spirit. What is your name?" His voice is fresh water lapping at the edges of my consciousness.

"You can call me legion because we are an army!" My mouth spits the words.

Just outside the graveyard lives a herd of swine. The demon hoard within me grasps at the hope those swine offer. Jesus tells them to go.

The sudden silence in my head is deafening.

There is chaos all around as the vast sea of swine explodes into motion. They run every which way until one breaks out toward the cliff. Then another follows, and the next, until the entire herd stampedes toward the precipice. Their keepers stand back in horror and shock, trying to decide what they should do. Then they run off toward town in a panic.

But my panic is over! I am cured!

Cured isn't the half of it. There must be a better word for what happened to me. I'm healed. I'm whole. I'm delivered. I'm free. I feel clean. That's it . . . I am clean—perhaps for the first time ever! Clean on the inside; clean on the outside. All the filth that spewed from my mouth, the dark cloud over my mind, the bitter water that was my daily drink—all gone in an instant.

My darkness now noonday light, exposing what? Exposing a new me, and there is nothing ugly left. He made me beautiful.

"Lord, let me come with You. I want to be Your disciple. I want to follow You, go where You go, hear Your words, move in Your circle. May I come with You?"

Jesus looks at me. There is such life, such strength, in His gaze. He says:

"Go home to your own people. Tell them your story—what the Master did, how he had mercy on you."

And so I stand before you today, my people—clean, clothed, in my right mind—to tell you about this man, Jesus, who was not afraid of me. He saw *me*, not what I had become. He saw me. He touched me. He changed me. He cleaned me. He loved me.

Will you follow Him with me?

~~~

To read the original story, see Mark 5:1-20 and Luke 8:26-39.

"Prepare God's arrival! Make the road smooth and straight!
Every ditch will be filled in, every bump smoothed out,
the detours straightened out, all the ruts paved over.
Everyone will be there to see the parade of God's salvation."
Luke 3:4-6

My Dear John

Elizabeth

Today I feel too old. I know my old age is a blessing, but today I'm sure I have lived too long.

No one should have to sit for her own child's mourning. No mother should hear the news I heard today. The day you hear of your own son's execution is the day you are too old.

I remember like it was yesterday the day my husband, Zachariah, came home and could not speak. He completed his service at the temple, and when he returned home, he was all waving and shrugging and nodding and pointing, but didn't utter a word.

At first he tried to explain using hand motions and gestures, but finally he sat down and wrote out what had happened to him in the holy place. He said he could not speak because he did not believe what the angel said in the temple, yet he seemed full of expectation.

We long ago stopped trying to have children. In fact, it had been five years since I abandon my pleas for a child. For ten years before that, I prayed Hannah's prayer every month, and every month, no change.

Let me tell you, that night it was as though we were twenty-five again. We were young and in love, without the fear that it wouldn't work or the shame and blame of fault and failure. It was like the first time.

And it did not take a month to figure it out either. The next morning, I knew God had created a miracle in my body. Zachariah's voiceless joy was infectious. I didn't even have to tell him. He knew, too. We were going to have a child, a son—a son with a destiny.

The memory fixed itself deep within him. Those words etched themselves on the silent walls of his heart, the words the angel spoke to my Zach in the temple. He never let one of them fall to the ground. The day he arrived home from the temple he wrote them, and he made me read them aloud to him every day until John was born:

"Don't fear, Zachariah. Your prayer has been heard. Elizabeth, your wife, will bear a son by you. You are to name him John. You're going to leap like a gazelle for joy, and not only you—many will delight in his birth. He'll achieve great stature with God.

"He'll drink neither wine nor beer. He'll be filled with the Holy Spirit from the moment he leaves his mother's womb. He will turn many sons and daughters of Israel back to their God. He will herald God's arrival in the style and strength of Elijah, soften the hearts of parents to children, and kindle devout understanding among hardened skeptics—he'll get the people ready for God."

Could the queasy feeling in my belly be Elijah, for whom we always set a place at the table? Was this the one who would make a way for Messiah to come?

We hid ourselves away when I began to show. I was so pleased my shame was gone, but I did not want to be a spectacle. I did let my family know, especially my young cousin, Mary. She was such a sweet young girl. Back when I thought I would never be a mother, my mother's sister gave birth to a daughter, Mary, and we spent many Sabbaths together. I thought she was the closest I would come to having my own child.

About six months into my time, I received a letter from Mary saying she and her betrothed, Joseph, wanted to visit. She said she had news to share.

When I think back on that day, I still remember the sensation I felt when Mary walked through the door. It was the baby in my womb. At the sound of Mary's voice, the baby nearly left me. The Spirit of God overwhelmed me. The sensation of peace, of total shalom, overtook me, as though everything that had ever been wrong was right.

Just the memory of it lightens the sorrow I feel today.

The boys, who recognized each other in the womb, would spend their childhoods together. They would laugh and play. They would talk and even pray. There were never two boys like them. There was joy and childishness, but there were times when they were so sober. And their questions! What questions they would ask!

Then my John left home, but not to go to the city or to work in the temple. He went to live alone in the wilderness. From time to time he would visit, and I hardly recognized him.

"Are you eating?" I would ask.

"Momma, don't worry. God provides for me," he would answer.

"You look like you are starving."

But he stayed out in the wilderness.

The first time I heard news about my boy was when the local congregation headed out to the wilderness to see "the prophet." The men in town got together to investigate the reports of this prophet who was preaching beside the Jordan.

They said he was unshaven and unkempt. He called the nation to repent and walk through the waters of baptism as a declaration of its devotion to the One God.

I went out to see, and I let my son baptize me. The shalom I'd felt the day Mary came was still strong around him as he ministered there in the wilderness.

The next news I heard of my son was that he was in prison. It seems he didn't restrain his message of repentance, even before the king. King Herod threw him in jail for the sake of his wife. John did not approve of Herod's relationship with the wife of his brother, Philip. Unwilling to compromise, he shined light on the depths of Herod's sin.

Today I received heartbreaking news of him again. My son, John, my beautiful boy, his body lies in a dark prison, and his head is in the court of the king. How could they mutilate him so, my dear John, my son of promise, my miracle.

~~~

To read the original story, see Matthew 14:1-12, Mark 6:17-28, Luke 1:5-25, 1:57-80, and Luke 3.

Jumping out of the boat,
Peter walked on the water to Jesus.
Matthew 14:29

MASTER, IF IT'S YOU

PETER

I've never seen anything impact Him like the news we got this morning. John was dead, John the Baptist. And not just dead—murdered, decapitated by that tyrant, Herod. He was visibly shaken when He heard the news.

All He wanted to do was get away—away from the crowds, away from the city, away from us. Away. He needed to take in this sadness, to process this loss. He no doubt wanted to talk to His Father about it. That's where He, Jesus, turned when . . . well, just about any time. When stress was bearing down, when decisions had to be made, even when He was full of joy, He went to the Father.

We'd all been out in the towns and villages. He had sent us two by two, and, well, we had some stories to tell. Andrew and I were amazed, and as the others began to arrive, the stories kept growing. Matthew and Thomas were telling a story about casting a demon out in Capernaum. James was relating how he and Bart laid hands on a woman's eyes, and she saw for the first time in her life. We were all laughing and rejoicing as we shared our own accounts.

Then Philip came in with the news about John, and the tone of the gathering changed abruptly. Jesus got quiet. Everyone got quiet.

"Let's get out of here," He said.

He headed down to the boat, and we all followed. He asked me to navigate to a secluded place, away from the cities and towns and multitudes. We'd been there often to be alone with the Master. There we had laughed and learned for hours on end without interruption. But it was not going to be like that today. The word was out, and huge numbers of men, women, and children were there to meet us as we disembarked.

I don't know if the crowds grew because we were all doing His works now, spreading His name—His fame—in the region, or if those who opposed us were just sending the mobs in order to get under His skin. Either way, as always, He took immediate control of the situation.

He settled in, the rock embankment at His back creating a natural amphitheater, and began to teach. As He did so, the assembly continued to grow. It was late afternoon, and we had not even had lunch. As the sun began its descent, I pressed my way over to Jesus and suggested He should wrap it up.

"We're out in the country and it's getting late. Dismiss the people so they can go to the villages and get some supper."

He turned to look at me. The twinkle in His eye asked, "Ready for your next lesson?"

"There is no need to dismiss them. You give them supper."

His words tossed me like a wave of distress.

"Me? I didn't bring any food. I didn't even know we were coming across the lake. If we go and buy food, it will cost a year's wages. There have to be 5,000 men here, and most of them have their wives and kids. How could I possibly feed—"

Jesus put His hand on my shoulder and said, "Peter, Peter, just have them sit in groups of fifty. What food do we have?"

Thomas came up with a tiny satchel.

"There was a boy who had a couple fish and some bread, maybe five little loaves. But what good is that among all these?"

"Bring them here," Jesus said.

And isn't that always the answer?

"Jesus, there is a man here with a withered hand."

"Bring him to Me."

"Jesus, my son is sick."

"Bring him to Me."

"Jesus, my daughter's dead."

"Bring Me to her."

He took the bread and lifted it up toward heaven and gave thanks. Then He broke off a piece of bread and fish for each of the twelve of us and told us to share what we had.

I went to my first group of fifty and handed my entire stash of lunch to the first person. I watched in astonishment as each person took some and passed it. When it came back to me, I was sure it was larger than when I started. As I went on to the next group, I noticed the first fifty were all busy eating.

As we passed the food around, the din began to rise. Astonishment ran amuck in the crowd. Many were there to see a miracle; some came to hear Him teach, and I am sure some were there to undermine Him, to get some bit of dirt. But now all were eating—eating this heaven-sent fish sandwich—and there wasn't a naysayer in the bunch.

When the feasting was over, Jesus told us to gather up the leftovers and take them down to the boat. He said He would meet us back across the lake. We gathered up twelve baskets full of scraps. Some of the scraps were the size of my original portion.

I looked back as we headed down to the boat, and I saw Jesus touching people as they left—a handshake, a touch on the shoulder, a pat on the back. I know He wanted to be alone, but Jesus always gave all of Himself when He was with others.

As we cast off, I could see Him heading up the mountain, where He could be alone. I expect He poured His heart out to His Father. I had almost forgotten about John, with all that had transpired since our reunion that morning.

It was night by now, and as we headed out into the Sea of Galilee, the waves grew. The sky began to anger, or so it seemed, as the star-specked black turned to a foreboding gray. In short order, the wind whipped up, and the waves pounded us.

We pulled at the oars for hours, making little headway. Eight of us would pull for a quarter hour while the others rested; then, four would step in and four more rest. But the night, the wind, the waves . . . They would not end.

Andrew, on a rowing break, looked out into the night.

"What's that?" he said.

At first we all ignored him. I was exhausted. It had to be four watch, and I was not in the mood for sightseeing.

"No, really," Andrew said, more insistent this time. "What— or should I say who—is that?"

I rested my oar and turned my head to see what he was squawking about. Sure enough, off the port side of the stern, perhaps fifty cubits out, I could barely make out the form of a man. As we drifted, pounded by the waves, we all stared in wonder.

Someone let down the anchor so we would not end up back at the shore. As I heard the chain running, James yelled out exactly what I was thinking.

"Is it a ghost?"

"Whoever it is, He walks like Jesus," John shouted above the commotion.

Then Bart said, "I think He is going to walk right by!"

The figure was now almost to the bow of the boat but still about thirty cubits off.

"Master?" I called out.

It was only then that He turned toward the boat and walked toward us.

Walked toward us?

It rose up in me—I'm not sure why—but the next thing I knew, I was calling out to Him again.

"Master, if it's really you, call me to come to you on the water."

He was just close enough for me to see His face, its ready-for-the-next-lesson expression so familiar to me.

"Come ahead."

When I think back on what happened next, I shake my head. The rest of the men stood in stunned silence, staring, but I pulled off my coat, climbed up on the gunwale, and into—or should I say onto—the waves I went.

As I looked at Jesus, He stopped coming toward me and held out His arms to me like a father welcoming a toddling child. His eyes were saying, "Come on, come on! You can do it!" Then all at once, a wave smacked my back, and I turned to take a quick look.

That was when I started to sink. But Jesus reached down and grabbed my hand. He looked at me and shook His head. For a minute, I thought He was going to drag me through the water and back to the boat, but then He pulled me up, and we walked back to the boat together.

As soon as He stepped onto the boat, the sea settled down.

When I looked around at the boys, they were all on their knees.

"You really are the Son of God!" Andrew said. "Amen!" we all cried, as what had just happened penetrated our hearts and minds.

As each day passes, I am more in awe of Jesus..

Truly, He is the Christ, the Son of the living God.

~~~

To read the original story, see Matthew 14, Mark 6:14-54, and John 6:1-21.

"Your daughter is no longer disturbed.
The demonic affliction is gone."
Mark 7:29

CRUMBS FOR A DOG

SYROPHOENICIAN WOMAN

My daughter turned ten yesterday. We celebrated with other girls her age. I never thought this day would come. I thought she would be dead by the time she was eight.

We live in Tyre now, but we came here from Damascus. My parents had a mixed marriage, making me half Syrian and half Phoenician. We faced prejudice in every area of our lives. My father couldn't keep a job for long. At the first sign of trouble, they fired him, sent him packing. My mother could not work at all, since she had strong Phoenician features. I grew up in Damascus, and my husband and I decided to raise our family there.

I will admit I was afraid to raise a child in what I knew would be a hard world for her. I hated to saddle her with a life filled with the same racial bias and abuse I had faced growing up.

But when I saw her, when I looked into my Coriander's beautiful eyes and felt her tiny grip on my index finger, my fears melted away.

For the next six years, we lived the life of my dreams. My husband got a steady job working for a mason, and I did some cleaning for neighbors, Coriander always in tow.

Then the trouble started. Cori began to misbehave. At first it was no big deal. She was a child, and we wrote it off as pressing to find the boundaries. You know how kids will explore their environment to see where the edges are.

But we soon knew something more was going on. She had changed. Her sweetness was gone, as was any submission. She no longer reacted to punishment with anything but further rebellion.

She began to use language I had never even heard, and I know she hadn't. I had to ask my husband what some of the words meant, and sometimes he wouldn't even tell me. Where was this coming from?

After a few months, we took her to some local holy men to see what they could do for us. We tried the Greek temples. We tried the Hebrew temples. We even tried those frightening witches who meet in the groves late at night.

It only made things worse. The more we tried, the worse she got, until finally my husband told me he could not allow such evil to stay in his house. He turned us out.

That's when I made my way to Tyre. We've lived here for two years now, and all I can do is beg for food and keep my daughter locked up and hidden. She's out of control. Sometimes she'll lash out at me, and sometimes she tries to kill herself. Every once in a while I get a glimpse of my little girl, but it's fleeting at best.

I've been hearing tales coming from Galilee and the south of a healer roaming the Jewish countryside. I've tried the Jews, and they were no help, but if I dare believe the stories, this man is even raising the dead. If He could raise that woman's boy in Nain, He could bring my daughter back, too.

Desperation had me like a vise, and when I heard Jesus, the Healer, was right here in Tyre, I had to find a way to reach Him.

I heard He was in a house, trying to get away from the crowds. I managed to find a back entrance and snuck into the room where He and His disciples were reclining. As I entered the room, I found myself standing behind Him. I got just close enough to be sure He would hear me. In the sweetest voice I could muster through my distress, I said:

"Mercy, Master, Son of David! My daughter is cruelly afflicted by an evil spirit."

I wasn't sure He heard me the first time, so I repeated myself.

He never gave the slightest indication He heard me at all, even though I was standing less than a cubit away from Him.

I said it once more.

"Mercy, Master, Son of David! My daughter is cruelly afflicted by an evil spirit."

One of the men who attended Him looked over his shoulder at me.

"Now she's bothering us. Would you please take care of her? She's driving us crazy," he said to the Master.

Then He turned and looked at me, really saw me for the first time. I wondered what He would do. Would He be like my husband and send me away to fend for myself? Would He be like the other religious men I approached who would not soil themselves with an outsider? I raised my eyes to His and saw in them a concern, a compassion I had not known before.

"I was sent only to save the lost sheep of Israel."

He sounded sad when He said it, like He wanted to help but didn't have permission to do so.

As I looked into His eyes, I saw past this man who stood before me. Don't ask me to explain, but there was something—a greatness— something wonderful behind His eyes. I fell to my knees before Him and worshipped.

"Master, help me."

When I first came in, I was ready to demand His help, but kneeling in His presence, awe overtook me. The longer I knelt before Him, the more His presence impacted me. I began to tremble. I was not worthy to come before this man.

He spoke again.

"It's not right to take bread out of children's mouths and throw it to dogs."

If anyone else had said that to me, it would have hurt. Another slap in the face. But coming from Him, I knew I had no right, no entitlement, to special treatment. And yet there was compassion in the air, drawing me in, bidding me come and ask again.

"You're right, Master, but beggar dogs do get scraps from the master's table."

All was silent for a moment, and then He laughed. He wasn't mocking me. It was more like my words found their way through a crack in a wall. Not a wall of His making or mine, but a wall that separated us nonetheless. My humility mingled with His compassion dissolved the boundary that seconds ago stood as a roadblock to my salvation.

His laughter was infectious. Soon I was laughing, too, as were all the men who stood with Him.

"Oh, woman, your faith is something else. What you want is what you get!"

There was a glee in His voice, a delight, as though granting my deepest need gave Him His deepest joy.

Part of me didn't want to go. Part of me wanted to bask in this peace, this wonder. Then I thought of my daughter. I saw her in my mind's eye— whole, well, and in her right mind.

I ran. I sprinted through the streets to the place I had left her. I burst through the door, and there she was. I could see it in her eyes. My little girl was back! The sweet child who left me four years earlier was in my arms again.

This all happened about a month ago. Today, I am working for a tailor here in Tyre, and my daughter is going to school with the other children her age. We have our life back, thanks to Jesus the Messiah.

~~~

To read the original story, see Matthew 15:21-28 and Mark 7:24-30.

> *"...my Father is right now offering you
> bread from heaven, the real bread."*
> John 6:32-33

Eat My Flesh

Reluctant Follower

Eat My flesh? Drink My blood?

I have been following this Jesus for a few months now. The first time I heard Him teach, He was on the hillside in Galilee telling us stories. They were simple farming tales of men with fields and seeds. They were tales of sowing and reaping.

Unlike the rabbis in the synagogue, He talked as though He knew God personally. To Him, God was not an outsider. He made me feel as though I, too, could know "the Father," as He called Him.

Then yesterday, all the way across the Sea of Galilee, we listened to Him teach again. This time He spoke about stewarding that which the Father had given us. He fed the whole crowd. There had to be thousands there. Many I recognized from other gatherings around this wise man.

Some are calling Him Messiah, and I'm beginning to hope they're right. The food He gave us yesterday would have cost the better part of a year's wages, though I didn't see where He got it. We all ate our fill, and there were scraps of bread and fish everywhere.

Early this morning, I heard He had made His way back across the lake, so we headed over to see if we could find Him. It's not too difficult these days, as there are rarely fewer than a thousand followers.

When we got to the other side, He was teaching again, and it looked like the same crowd. All five thousand made their way around or across the lake to hear Him again today.

He started talking about the bread from yesterday, saying we were just following Him for the food. Well, I know the crowd is growing, so I suppose some of these folks are just here for the food or for what they can get out of it. But that's not me. I'm not like that. I'm here for the teaching. I'm here because He speaks with authority. I'm not like the others, the thrill seekers.

Somebody called out, "Moses gave us bread from heaven. What sign do you show us?"

That's when it started to get weird. He said it was not Moses but His Father who gave us the manna, and that *He* was the bread the Father had given.

Yesterday He gave us bread to eat, and today He's telling us He is the bread. He said He came down from heaven, but I heard He grew up in Nazareth. Next He said if we ate His flesh we would live forever.

Eat His flesh? This is just what I was afraid of. He must be crazy!

And it didn't end there. Not only did He tell us His flesh was the food the Father had given us, He said if we wanted to live, we had to drink His blood!

I don't get it.

Up till now, He's always been so practical, so down to earth. But all this talk about eating flesh and drinking blood has got me wondering if I'm following the wrong man. I've given two months of my life to follow this Jesus, but I just can't see carrying on any longer. He asks too much. I can't just overlook these outbursts. It saddens my heart to walk away, but it sounds like the Jews are right; He's just another pretender.

I thought He was the One.

~~~

To read the original story, see John 6.

"Woman, where are they? Does no one condemn you?"
"No one, Master."
"Neither do I," said Jesus. "Go on your way. From now on, don't sin."
John 8:10-11

EXPOSED

ADULTEROUS MAN

How has it come to this? I'm standing here with a rock in my hand amidst all this anger. The anger is not mine, but I can feel it. It's all around.

I didn't see this coming as I sat at breakfast with my wife, Anna, and my two little ones. I think of myself as a good father, a good husband. I have a steady job working with the dairyman. We sell our milk from a cart near the sheep gate. I almost have enough saved to buy a few cows of my own.

But at noontime, as I sat in the square eating the lunch my Anna had packed for me, I saw her. I have known her for a few months. I say *known,* but not really, though our eyes have met often. The few words we have traded have been suggestive and flirtatious, but it meant nothing.

When I first saw her, the words of my father rang in my ears. On my wedding day he told me I must be like Job and make a covenant with my eyes if I wanted to be faithful to my Anna. But that day, my eyes saw only my sweet bride, and I can remember thinking such evil could never tempt me.

The day I first saw this woman in the market, she caught me staring. I looked away immediately, but I felt temptation's net, and it had me. The next time, I let my eyes linger a bit longer.

Once I saw her walking through the temple gate with a man I took to be her father. I later learned it was her husband. Not a great match for her.

Today, she walked right up to where I was eating and sat down beside me. I told her she should not sit next to me right there in the square because people would whisper.

"I just need someone to talk to," she said, right on the edge of tears. "Where can I talk with you?"

I took her to a place I knew would be empty and quiet at that time of day, and she began to cry in earnest. She told me of her life, and at first I just listened. I told myself she needed me to listen. She needed a friend. She just needed to talk about it. I needed to be compassionate, to listen like a friend.

Soon I was holding her as she sobbed and trembled.

The rest is a blur. What started as a comforting touch became an embrace, and soon I found myself overwhelmed. Compassion became passion, and the next thing I knew, the door burst open.

A group of men broke in, some in religious robes, including my own rabbi. This rabbi had married Anna and me; he had circumcised my little Yacob. They grabbed us and started dragging us out into the square.

"Let the boy go," my rabbi said. "I know him."

The woman's husband was among our intruders. "You Jezebel! You harlot!" he yelled in our wake.

I followed the angry group out into the square, where they had gathered up stones. I'd lived in Jerusalem my whole life, but I'd never seen anyone stoned in the streets. We read about it in the Law of Moses, but we never took it that far. My rabbi stood beside me. He bent down and picked up two stones. They were bigger than a man's fist. He took my right hand and forced me to take the cold, hard lump of hatred.

I dropped it, but he reached down, picked it up, and gave it back to me.

"If you will not do this thing, you will be up there with her," he said to me. I could hardly breathe.

Then the crowd swelled forward. One of the rabbis called out, "Jesus is in the outer court. Follow me, and let's hear what that upstart will have us do with her."

Soon the woman lay face down in the dust. I could still hear her sobs. Before her stood a man dressed in common robes. There was already a good-size crowd with Him before we pushed our way through.

"Teacher, this woman was caught red-handed in the act of adultery. Moses, in the Law, gives orders to stone such persons. What do you say?"

It was then I realized this was not about the woman, or about her sin, or about the law. It was a test for this preacher. It was not the woman in the dirt who was on trial here. It was this Jesus. This was a test for Him. They wanted to see what He would do.

Would this so-called Son of Man side with the sinner, or would He side with the religious leaders? They hated the title He had taken. They worked so hard to be more than mere men. These priests, scribes, and Pharisees craved the esteem of men; they were anything but common.

But this Jesus, He would eat with sinners. He was not ashamed to be with them in their homes and in the streets. How would He deal with this woman? Would He take her part and defy the Lord God's own law? Would He take up a stone with us and break faith with the people?

This had me nervous. If He took up the law, I might just be next.

As I stood, stone in hand and awaiting His judgment, I thought back to those glances that brought me to this place. I wasn't so innocent. A place in my heart had sought out this adultery. I allowed my eyes to draw me into dissatisfaction with a life full of blessing.

Jesus positioned Himself between those of us with stones and the woman. She was still weeping with her face in the dirt. He knelt down and wrote something in the dust.

I could not see what He was writing, but, in the silence my guilt and shame were mounting. Again I heard my father's words: "Remember son," he would say, "Hell and destruction are never full, so man's eyes are never satisfied."

How had I fallen so far? How could this man expose my heart without speaking one word?

Then He stood and looked at us—at me!

"The sinless one among you, go first: Throw the stone," He said.

After a moment, He got back down in the dirt with the woman. As He continued to write in the dust, His finger tracing the law in my heart, I saw for the first time the wickedness of my actions.

And I was not the only one. First the elders began to back off, some dropping their stones, others taking them away as they quietly pulled back from the crowd.

As I stood there, I could hear my own voice speaking my vows to dear Anna those eight years ago. What I wanted to do was fall down and beg Him to forgive me. That's when I had to leave. I wanted to run, but I just dropped the stone and backed away. My sin, my unfaithfulness, filled my heart. I had to be rid of it. But how? How could I be free of this guilt? I never knew this darkness of guilt and shame until I stood in the presence of such holiness, such wisdom, such purity.

Who is this man?

What must I do to be saved from this condemnation that fills my heart?

~~~

To read the original story, see John 8:1-11.

*"A man named Jesus made a paste and
rubbed it on my eyes and told me,
'Go to Siloam and wash.' I did what he said.
When I washed, I saw."*
John 9:11

THE SOUND OF SHAME

BLIND MAN

I know that sound. I know it all too well. Someone is spitting again. It has become a part of everyday life for me. Such hypocrisy and self-righteousness. It makes me sick.

Just because I stand beside the road holding a sign does not make me less than human. The Lord knows I have tried holding onto a job, but there is little a blind man can do in Nazareth. I've never married and don't expect I ever will. I live with my parents, and that in itself seems to carry shame.

I hear them approaching. It's not just a couple men out for a walk after the assembly. It sounds like every man in Nazareth is coming. Perhaps the whole synagogue put down their scrolls and headed right toward me. As they approach, it has the clamor of a mob, but when they stop in front of me, a hush comes over them.

Then the one to the right—he has the voice of a squirrel—asks that horrible, ignorant question. It is the question I have heard all my life; it makes me wonder if there can be a God at all.

"Rabbi, who sinned: this man or his parents, causing him to be born blind?"

How often I have cried out to God, "Why me? Why my sight?" But when this Sabbath crowd makes its way from the synagogue, their questions—accusations—cut me.

What sort of sin could I commit in my mother's womb? What sort of lifestyle would my parents have to live to deserve a blind son? What kind of God would punish me for something my parents did before I was born?

Just the sound of this ignorant man asking such a question makes my face hot. It stirs up my anger. And then I hear it—the sound of someone getting ready to spit.

They pretend they spit to display their godly hatred for sin, but to me it feels a lot like their ungodly hatred for me. Sometimes they ride by on their horses and don't even stop; they just spit on me from aloft. So ingrained is their prejudice, so deep their indifference to my plight, they give me nothing but their spittle and the back end of their horses.

At this, one at the head of the crowd draws in saliva to let his contempt for me find a place on my tattered clothes. I brace myself for the impact. I know it won't add to the pain I feel on the outside, still his contempt for me does add to my own self-loathing. As they demonstrate their distaste for my sins for all to see, I wonder if they spit in the mirror when they look into their own self-righteous eyes in the morning.

This is strange. I hear the spit but do not feel it. What's going on? Then I pick up the conversation taking place right in front of me.

I hear Him say it wasn't my sin, and it wasn't the sin of my parents. Someone in the crowd calls out the name I have been hearing for weeks now—Jesus. Could this be Him, the man I have been hearing about? Crowds healed. Multitudes fed. Is this *that* Jesus?

Then Jesus spoke.

"You're asking the wrong question. You're looking for someone to blame. There is no such cause-effect here. Look instead for what God can do. We need to be energetically at work for the One who sent me here, working while the sun shines. When night falls, the workday is over. For as long as I am in the world, there is plenty of light. I am the world's Light."

I didn't understand what He was talking about, but the next thing I know, there is some kind of paste in my eyes. He spits in the dust, makes mud, and puts it in both of my eyes.

This is not making any sense to me. I have heard such wonderful stories of this man from Nazareth, and now I have mud in my eyes. It's bad enough when people spit on me, but this? This is . . . wait! It's getting hot. It's burning! What has He done to me?

Jesus spoke again. *"Go, wash in the pool of Siloam."*

He wants me to walk two miles to a filthy, stagnant pool and wash my eyes out? I can't decide what to do. I could go to my house and be back in no time, but He wants me to head all the way to the other end of town.

Is this just an elaborate insult?

I have heard such amazing stories about this Jesus, but I have not heard of any others walking around with mud in their eyes.

And yet, somewhere deep inside there is a "yes" rising up.

What do I have to lose?

So I'll go.

"Are you coming with me?" I ask, but while I was flip-flopping back and forth, Jesus had moved on.

Many from His crowd stay, though. They want to see what I will do. They want to see a miracle. They have more hope than I do. But then, they are not the ones setting themselves up for ridicule when I wash my eyes clean and find I am still in the dark.

So I head down to the pool. I am drawn along with the crowd, which is a blessing since it is not the easiest place to negotiate with the lights out.

By the time I get there, the mud has dried, but the heat has not subsided. If anything, it has increased. I half expect a sizzle when I put my head in the water.

I dunk down and give my head a shake. When I come up, most of the mud is gone, but my eyes are still stuck closed. And yet it was the strangest sensation! Is this what light is like? Even with my eyes closed, I knew I could see. This darkness ends today!

I go under again, barely containing my emotion. I can see! I was blind, and now I see! I spent a lifetime in a prison without even a shadow, and today . . . light!

Now my eyes are fully open. I don't know what to say. People who have seen me begging on the roadside for decades are coming up and saying, "Aren't you the blind man? Don't I know you? Where have I seen you before?"

All I can think to say today is, "I was blind, but now I see!"

~~~

To read the original story, see John 9:1-11.

*"I'd say it's easier for a camel to go through
a needle's eye than for the rich to get into God's kingdom."*
Mark 10:25

WHAT AM I LACKING?

RICH YOUNG RULER

Growing up with wealth, I never thought much about the things that worry other people. I can't remember ever being hungry or wondering whether another meal was in the offing. I never wore secondhand clothes.

My father was wealthy, and I'm not talking about money. Sure, there was always money, but money is a by-product of wealth. Many people get that turned around. They think, "If I only had ten thousand denarii, I'd be set." What they don't get is that wealth produces money. The lands my father passed into my hands and the herds and flocks I own produce all I could ever need.

I am always well dressed, and when I'm out and about, I usually have a few of my closest and dearest servants with me. I have always been able to afford entertainment. I can lay down enough coin to buy some happiness, but there has always been an empty place deep within me.

Recently, one of my attendants, a Jew like me, experienced something that changed him. Don't misunderstand—there was nothing wrong with him before. He was always on time and faithful to me. He was trustworthy, and I could allow him to handle my money and manage my holdings.

But one day when he came into my presence, he . . . I don't know. He just lit up. When I asked him about it, he told me he'd been passing through town and stumbled upon a crowd. His curiosity drew him in, and the words he heard held him there.

He said, "Now I am a disciple of Jesus." He asked me if I would allow him to spend time listening to Jesus's teachings while He was in town.

I have to tell you, he was so different. For the first time, I felt he had something I didn't. He kept talking about eternal life and living water.

Though he was an indentured servant and subject to my command, he seemed to stand in greater freedom than I.

Since he said this man, this Jesus, was going to be in town for a few more days, I told him we could go together to hear Him talk.

When we arrived, He was having a conversation with the Jewish leaders, and it seemed like they were laying a trap for Him. They were pressing Him with leading questions. It was an obvious attempt to discredit Him in front of His rather large following.

I couldn't hear the whole conversation, but the leaders from the synagogue walked away perturbed. As they left, the crowd began to press Him. Women sent their children in to touch this Jesus. I could tell His entourage was getting upset with the way people were crowding Him. But He put His hands on each of the children as they came to Him and spoke a blessing over each one. No two of the blessings were alike. He was speaking into their future and creating a path for them to follow. I was so impressed with every word He uttered. He never wavered, but spoke with a profound authority. My parents never spoke into my life like that. Yet here is this man from Nazareth picking up the children of total strangers and giving them a destiny. It was wonderful to behold!

I wanted Him to speak into my life. I wanted the eternal life my servant spoke of. I wanted Jesus to speak words of hope over me. The child inside me cried out for His touch.

Before I thought better of it, I dashed right into the middle of everything, fell to my knees before Him, and revealed what was in my heart.

"Good Teacher, what must I do to get eternal life?"

There I was, on my knees before Him, feeling quite foolish and just a little hopeful.

He looked at me—honestly, it felt more like a probe than a look—and He said:

"Why are you calling me good? No one is good, only God."

I got the impression He was asking me if I thought He was God. I grew up in a good Jewish home. I know the Lord God is One. But He kept speaking.

"If you want to enter the life of God, just do what he tells you. You know the commandments . . ."

The commandments. Excellent! I grew up in the home of a Jewish businessman. From a young age, the commandments were pounded into my brain. Business is built on trust, and wealth flows from righteousness. We read the proverbs over and over, and the commandments hung on the kitchen wall.

"Which ones?" I asked Him.

He started to list them:

"Don't murder, don't commit adultery, don't steal, don't lie, honor your father and mother, and love your neighbor as you do yourself."

As He was listing, I was counting to myself and trying to figure out which ones He missed. But when He finished, I told Him I had always kept the commandments. I was beginning to feel like this whole conversation was kind of strange. I thought He was going to speak a blessing over me. I thought He was going to receive me with open arms. I thought He would be eager to have such an important and outstanding follower. Why were we talking about me keeping the commandments? You know how things race through your mind.

"Teacher, I have—from my youth—kept them all!" I said. "What am I lacking?"

He got quiet for a minute, and then a new look crossed His face. What was it? Love? Compassion? Pity? Sorrow?

"There's one thing left: Go sell whatever you own and give it to the poor. All your wealth will then be heavenly wealth. And come follow me."

Now I got quiet. Was this a joke? A trick? A test? Sell it all and then just give the money away? And to the poor, no less. I am okay with giving alms. In fact, a portion of my earnings is set aside every year for the poor. But to give the indigent great sums of money can create an entitlement mentality. It undermines their ambition. It's not a good idea. Why doesn't Jesus know this?

Besides, how would I live? These guys look like nomads. They travel constantly from place to place. They have no visible means of support, and I'm not sure I trust the one holding their money. You learn to get the measure of a man in my line of work.

What is He asking? Is He really demanding I just walk away from a fortune accumulated over the course of generations? What if I have children someday? What would I leave them? Didn't wise Solomon tell us to leave an inheritance to our children's children?

I'm not sure if He knew what I was thinking, but His gaze never faltered.

My eyes must have been asking what my heart was calculating, because He nodded.

"Everything."

My servant came over and helped me back to my feet. I turned away from this frustrating man. This was not how I expected the scenario to play out. I wanted what my servant had—that joy, peace, and freedom. But instead, my emptiness was deeper than ever.

To this day, I can't figure out if I rejected Him or He rejected me, but in the end, I know we both walked away saddened.

Occasionally I wonder if I could do it, if I could forsake all and follow Him. But I realize it would be like putting the very core of my being to death. He was asking me to turn away from my identity, from who I am.

I can't. I just can't.

~~~

To read the original story, see Matthew 19:16-31, Mark 10:17-31, and Luke 18:18-30.

"Then give Caesar what is his,
and give God what is his."
Matthew 22:21

POLL TAX PLOT

TEMPLE SERVANT

I can hardly believe I am asking this question. I resent this tax myself. Why were they having me ask this young upstart about the poll tax?

I work in the temple, mostly running errands for the Pharisees. I'm working as an intern in hopes of one day wearing those noble robes of authority.

These days they talk nonstop about this Jesus. He's been causing trouble in Jerusalem. Just this week, on the first day, He rode into the city with mobs thronging Him. The whole celebration had the feel of a king returning victorious from some great conquest.

Was it the same day or the next that He drove all the merchants out of the Court of the Gentiles? There is so much going on; I can't keep it straight in my mind. Anyway, that's what really clinched it for my mentor. He and a few of his fellows came up with this plan, and now I am an actor in a loathsome play.

I'm sent here with a Roman denarius to try to trap Jesus with words in front of His followers.

The Romans require every person in our nation to pay a poll tax as tribute to Caesar. The paying of this tax tells Rome we accept its rule and recognize Caesar as our king. No Jew likes paying this tax. It is an affront to our religion and an offense to the Lord Almighty. Unlike our own half-shekel temple tax, which pays for the upkeep of the holy temple in Jerusalem, this tax has no exemptions. Men, women, children, slaves, even the priests have to pay tribute to Caesar.

The only thing worse than the Romans who imposed this tax are the Jews who collect it. I spit on them.

As I said, I'm laying a trap for Jesus. Here's the plan: I am to go to Him when He is addressing a large crowd and ask Him about this hateful tax. If He says pay it, we can accuse Him of blasphemy for putting Caesar above God. If He says don't pay it, we can take Him to the Romans and accuse Him of sedition.

None of these upstarts—these men who come along claiming to be Messiah—have ever allowed their followers to pay tribute to Rome. They rise and fall, attempting to gain enough followers to revolt against both Rome and Jerusalem. My father tells me of a Judas of Galilee who lived a couple decades back. Rome killed him and all his followers for a revolt that arose over this very tax.

So, today I'm off to trap this so-called Messiah.

I've heard He does miracles, but I don't believe all the rumors.

I've also heard He is a brilliant teacher. My wife's brother was listening to Him teach a while back. He told me that after a full day of listening to this man speak and being astounded by His insights, this Jesus and His men provided a meal of bread and fish for everyone. The way he tells it, the crowd was massive, thousands. There were no carts selling food, no tents of preparation. His disciples simply sat them down and began passing food from one to another, until everyone ate their fill.

I'm not sure what I think about all that, but today I have a job to do. So I press my way to within calling distance and shout out to Him:

"Teacher, we know you have integrity, teach the way of God accurately, are indifferent to popular opinion, and don't pander to your students. So tell us honestly: Is it right to pay taxes to Caesar or not?"

This gets the crowd's attention. As I said, there is not a Jew in Jerusalem, in all Judea, who does not hate this tax.

He called back to me:

"Why are you playing these games with me? Why are you trying to trap me? Do you have a coin? Let me see it."

The crowd loosens up a bit and lets me make my way in front of Him. As I hand Him the coin, He holds it up and looks at it, making a show of it.

"This coin—whose image is this? And whose name is engraved on it?"

Now the whole crowd answers, in one voice:

"*Caesar!*" You can feel the disgust in our voices.

He flips it back to me in a nonchalant manner. As it spins through the air, He replies:

"*Then give Caesar what is his . . .*"

I snatch the coin out of the air, and our eyes meet. Now He sees only me and speaks directly to my soul.

"*. . . and give God what is His.*"

We are not talking about taxes anymore.

It's as much in His eyes as in His words.

From the day I was born, my abba told me I was made in the image, the likeness, of the Lord God. As a Jew, I carry the name of God. He marked me as His possession—engraved me— on the day of my circumcision, my eighth day. I bear the image and name of the Almighty.

This simple phrase "*[Give] to God the things that are His*" breaks me—my heart—today.

I must give my life as a tribute to the One who made me, the One who marked me.

Truly this Jesus is Messiah.

Come worship Him with me!

~~~

To read the original story, see Matthew 22:15-21, Mark 12:13-17, and Luke 20:20-26.

*"You don't have to wait for the End.
I am, right now, Resurrection and Life."*
John 11:25

TODAY WE LIVE

THOMAS

I thought we came here to die.

A few days ago, we heard Lazarus was sick. At first I was sure we would head down to Judea. We had been up in Gennesaret when Andrew first heard the news from a friend of Martha's.

She had sent word north hoping the Master would come back down and visit him in Bethany. Lazarus and his whole family had been so good to us. Every time we passed through Bethany they hosted us, and we often stayed at their home when we were in Jerusalem for the festivals.

When we were together, there was a special dynamic between Jesus and Lazarus. The Master always made time to get away alone with him. Jesus made a huge impact on everyone in that family.

When I think of the change in Mary, his sister, I'm still amazed. I didn't know her before, but she had a reputation around Jerusalem. I had heard stories about her. Everyone just assumed she needed to get married and submit to a husband's leadership. No one suspected seven demons lived within her. It was sad.

To see her now, you would never know. The Lord broke down that stronghold in her life and began to pour in love. He treated her with honor. He cared about her. She changed inside and out. The once loud and bawdy woman now loved nothing more than sitting at the Master's feet as He taught us.

Now they were calling us to come and help. There was a note of desperation in Martha's message. She was afraid for her brother's life.

The night we got the message, Jesus said, "This won't end in death. It will end with Father and Son receiving glory."

When He said that, I looked over at Peter. He was usually willing to ask the hard questions, but he put his finger to his lips and slowly shook his head.

Two days later, Jesus suggested we head back down to Judea. Last time we were in Jerusalem, they tried to kill all of us. Walking the streets of Judea with us was not for the faint of heart. I'm certain we were all thinking it, but it was James who came right out and asked, "Isn't that suicide? Last time they almost stoned You when You healed that blind man."

Then He said:

"Our friend Lazarus has fallen asleep. I'm going to wake him up."

At that, Judas chuckled and said:

"Master, if he's gone to sleep, he'll get a good rest and wake up feeling fine."

"Lazarus died."

Jesus said it, making plain the point we were all missing:

"And I am glad for your sakes that I wasn't there. You're about to be given new grounds for believing. Now let's go to him."

Everyone started talking at once. Peter didn't want to go at all, and John was talking with James. From where I stood, I couldn't tell what they were saying. I shrugged and said:

"Come along. We might as well die with him."

Have you ever had one of those moments when you raise your voice above the din so the crowd can hear, and, at the same time, everyone suddenly stops talking? That's what happened as I said it. Everyone just stared at me.

So I said it again, quietly this time.

"We might as well die with him.."

We left the next morning.

When we arrived, you could see that the mourning had been going on for days. Martha must have gotten word we were on our way, because she met us at the edge of town. When she reached Jesus, she fought to keep her tears at bay.

"Master, if You'd been here, my brother wouldn't have died. Even now, I know that whatever You ask God He will give You."

He said to Martha:

"Your brother will be raised up."

You could tell she had been crying, and His words set her off again. When she regained her composure, she mumbled:

"I know that he will be raised up in the resurrection at the end of time."

She said it as though reciting the day's lesson to her rabbi, but all conviction was held at bay.

Jesus took her right hand in His, and with His other hand He drew her eyes up. I never know what to say when I am faced with such grief, but the Master was not shaken by her weeping.

As she looked in His eyes, she calmed. He said to her:

"I am, right now, Resurrection and Life."

Then He continued, His words addressed to all of us:

"The one who believes in me, even though he or she dies, will live. And everyone who lives believing in me does not ultimately die at all."

Then He looked back into Martha's eyes.

"Do you believe this?"

She said to him:

"Yes, Master. All along I have believed that you are the Messiah, the Son of God who comes into the world."

We kept moving on toward the house. Martha ran ahead of us. As we approached, I began to get nervous. Some of the Jewish leaders who had been trying to kill Jesus were there, as well as plenty of others.

We were not yet in the yard, when Mary came to us. She fell at Jesus's feet and burst into tears. Her grief impacted Him; He was visibly moved by her sorrow.

Through her sobbing she managed to say:

"Master, if only you had been here, my brother would not have died."

It wasn't an accusation, exactly. We've all walked with Him for years now and seen Him heal hundreds of men and women. It wasn't like it was hard for Him or took any special energy. It was just what He did. So why not Lazarus? Why not this one He loved?

By now we were close enough to hear the wailing and crying of the others at the tomb. Again, He was noticeably moved by the sorrowful scene.

He lifted Mary to her feet and asked, "Where have you laid him?"

Martha rejoined us and took Him and Mary by the hand. "Come and see," the women said.

The grave site was a few hundred yards from where they lived, and many had come to mourn with them. When He saw the closed tomb, Jesus wept.

The Jews who had come out of Jerusalem to pay their respects saw His great love for Lazarus. They had not come to weep. They were there because it was expected of them —a matter of duty—not an act of love.

One of them turned it against Him, though. "This man opens strangers' eyes, but could not come and help His own friend. What kind of love is that?"

Jesus, still deeply moved, walked right up to the tomb.

"Go ahead, take away the stone."

Martha was standing beside Him. She leaned in and said, "Master, he's been in there four days. By now the odor would be unbearable."

He looked at her, and then turned so all could hear.

"Didn't I tell you that if you believed, you would see the glory of God?"

Martha went over and asked a few of her neighbors to move the stone.

With His back to the tomb, Jesus turned His eyes to the heavens and began to pray.

"Father, I'm grateful that you have listened to me. I know you always do listen, but on account of this crowd standing here I've spoken so that they might believe that you sent me."

Then He turned and faced the tomb, and in a voice like a trumpet, He called out:

"Lazarus, come out!"

At first, the silence brought time to a screeching halt.

No one moved. I couldn't breathe.

Four days! What was He thinking?

Then there was a sound, a shuffling, and it was coming from the tomb. Next thing we knew, there stood Lazarus, wrapped head to toe in grave clothes.

Jesus looked at me and said, "Thomas, don't just stand there; you and Andrew unwrap him."

At that, the hillside erupted in shouts and cheers and laughter and singing and more shouts. Lazarus ran to Jesus and threw his arms around Him, and then Mary and Martha joined the embrace.

We all closed in on them, until the Master called out from the center, with laughter in His voice, to give them some air.

We all headed back to the house, where we feasted and talked, singing the praises of God and recounting the day.

In the middle of all the rejoicing, I stepped back and looked at Jesus. I have never known anyone who felt so deeply. He'd known just what He had planned from the beginning, and yet He mourned with those who mourned. Now He rejoiced at this life He had restored. No one knew as much joy as this man, nor as much sorrow.

I thought we came here to die, but today we live. And what a life we live when we walk with Jesus!

~~~

To read the original story, see John 11.

PASSION

*"When she poured this perfume on my body,
what she really did was anoint me for burial."*
Matthew 26:12

SOMETHING IN THE AIR

FRIEND OF SIMON

I can't believe it's actually happening. The Jewish spiritual leaders have been hounding Him for months, this Jesus, but I never thought it would come to this.

I have always hated crucifixions. Since the Romans have been in power here in my homeland, they like to do things their way. This is not punishment for crime; it is nothing more than public torture, with total humiliation thrown in for good measure. They tell me it makes the thieves and murderers think twice, but I can't see how any good can come of this.

The worst part is that because of my position, I am expected to attend every one of these horrid displays.

It's strange how my mind works, though. Today as I stand and watch this brutality, my mind keeps going back to the dinner party I went to last week. It must be something in the air. As Jesus stumbles through the streets on the way up to Golgotha's ugly crown, I catch a whiff of something, and I'm immediately back there again, back at Simon's house.

My boyhood friend, Simon, lives a short ride away in Bethany. As a Pharisee, he spends most of his days in Jerusalem, either in the temple or nearby. It wasn't long ago we were calling him Simon the Leper.

What a mess that was. A prominent Pharisee with a bright future, Simon always seemed to have everything going for him. But then I started to hear rumors about my old friend. I never saw him around town anymore. People said he was sick. One day, I ran into his boy, Judas, during one of the feast days, and he came right out and told me. Simon had leprosy.

He had to leave his family home in Bethany and live in the colony. You've probably noticed it a few furlongs outside the Dung Gate on the west side of the city, with all its ragged tents and open fires.

He's a brilliant man. As a boy, we called him Simon the Know-it-all or Smart Simon. He was a man on a mission for years—decades really—studying and networking to become Simon the Pharisee. Now they were calling him Simon the Leper.

It has been six months since the day he walked back into the temple to make the offerings Moses required for a cleansed leper. Only Simon would even know the law existed. Who would think to create a law for an impossible situation? None of the other priests or rabbis knew what to do. They had to scurry off and dig out the scrolls just to accept his offering and clear his name.

They may have cleared his name, but more often than not, folks call him Simon the Leper to this day.

My mind must be trying to block out the horror of what's happening right in front of me, because I keep picking up that smell.

You must be wondering how a man could be a leper one day and clean the next. Simon never gets tired of telling the story of the day Jesus and His ever-present entourage were heading into the city from the west. He was there with a group of nine other lepers, begging alms on the roadside. One of them in the group was a Samaritan. Leprosy breaks all boundaries. This Samaritan had heard that Jesus was a great healer. He called out to Him:

"Jesus, Master, have mercy on us!"

Soon they all joined in.

Simon tells me that Jesus looked over at them on the side of the road and said:

"Go, show yourselves to the priests."

Then He continued on His way. All ten men headed back toward their village. I'm not sure if any of them intended to go to the priests. According to Simon, as he walked away from Jesus he felt a sensation, like heat from the inside working its way out of his skin. In the places his disease was worst, the heat was strongest. As his Samaritan friend ran after Jesus, Simon went back to his tent.

It took no more than five minutes, and he was completely clean. He told me that at first he thought it must be some kind of trick, but the next morning he awoke and was still clean. He headed off to Jerusalem to show himself to the authorities.

They made him wait a full month before they would let him take up his office again, where he would have to interact with people. Once they received his offering, they allowed him to move back into his home.

Since the day he moved back home, he has been talking about throwing a party—a celebration to say thank you to Jesus for rescuing him from a life of shame and agony.

Today, leprosy seems like nothing as I watch this good man suffer. When I look at His bloody back, I wonder what on earth these Romans were thinking as they beat Him. Was there not one man to stand up and say "Enough!" as they tore Him apart? Instead, they jeered and taunted, crying out ugly epithets and insults.

There is definitely something in the air today . . . which draws me back to my story.

Simon threw a reception for Jesus. I guess you could call it that, since he invited everyone of importance. It was strange, what with all the stirrings against Jesus, to have Pharisees and Jesus's unkempt cadre under the same roof.

Simon wanted to find a way to show his appreciation for the healing he received, but it almost felt like a power play to me. I'm not sure which end of the table he was trying to impress, though. Was he trying to impress his temple friends with this huge spread, or was he going to try to broker peace between Jesus and the Pharisees?

I don't know what Simon was going for, but I know he did not want to see that woman in his house.

That's it! That's what I keep smelling, why I keep thinking about that night. It's the spikenard. I've gotten a whiff of it three times today, every time I get near Jesus. When they whipped Him, it's what I smelled. As He passed me in the streets during that unholy procession, I smelled it. And now, even from this distance, I can still smell the scent of that perfume.

It seemed like such a waste at the time for a woman like that, like Mary, to have such a thing, only to break it and pour it out on this man without reserve. It would have taken me a year's labor to buy such a gift for my wife.

What a spectacle! Weeping and blubbering her thanks to Him. One minute I thought she was talking to her Lover, the next to her Master, then to her King. Somehow she related to Him as Brother, Father, Husband, and Master. As I think back on the words she managed to mutter through her tears, it seems confused and disoriented. At the time, her words of adoration were beautiful. Her worship made her beautiful.

The smell of it, the spikenard, hung in the air. It was everywhere. I had to explain it to my wife when I got home that night because it clung to my clothes.

Even now, the smell of it brings to mind the strange beauty of Mary's worship. She was so completely abandoned to Him, and though she has a reputation, it didn't seem the least bit inappropriate. No, it had a purity about it, a cleanness I can't explain.

That's what I see looking back, but at the time . . . what a mess. Simon went crazy on her. I guess he was too caught up in trying to impress folks, so he tried to get her away from Jesus. He insulted and mocked her.

Her effrontery even upset some of Jesus's own followers. Everyone, it seemed, was up in arms. Some complained of the waste of a year's wages, some of the woman's reputation. Others murmured about the cloying fragrance itself; you could not get away from it in that enclosed place.

But today, as I watch this good man die, I can't help but think it was a fitting offering, a sweet savor to mask the stench of blood and gore. Today they took everything from Him except the remnants of her worship. Nothing else remained.

~~~

To read the original story, see Matthew 26:6-13, Mark 14:3-9, Luke 7:36-50, and 17:11-19.

"One of you is going to betray me."
John 13:21

UNCERTAINTY

JUDAS

This is just not going the way I thought it would. I have put almost three years of my life into this man's movement, and now He's getting all the wrong kind of attention.

At the start it was all so good. The night He calmed the storm, I thought for sure greatness awaited us just around the corner. There was talk amongst the men of finally throwing off Rome. If He could calm the sea, what are a few thousand Roman soldiers?

But now it seems everything He does just stirs up trouble. The Sanhedrin has put a price on His head, and I'm thinking I might just turn Him in. Maybe a night or two in stocks will help Him see that Rome is our enemy, not the temple.

And that sickly-sweet smell! I am so tired of the smell of that spikenard. It's been days, and everywhere we go the cloying smell hangs in the air. I can't believe He let the woman throw it all away. What a waste. We could have eaten for months on that pound of nard and ended the constant fish and bread.

What is He doing now?

I was hoping to slip out right after supper, but now He's up to something again. He has taken his tunic off, and it looks like He is putting on a servant's apron He found at the side of the room.

He has taken the basin of water, and now He's washing Philip's feet! Why? Why humiliate Himself like this? This is what's so frustrating about Jesus. One day we're following a would-be king, and the next day He's washing feet like a slave. In my father's house we pay people to wash the feet of our guests.

Now He's moved on to Thomas. Is He really going to take the time to wash everyone's feet? I need to get to the council meeting before they break up for the week, but I can hardly leave while He has everyone's attention.

As He washes Matthew's feet, just to my left, I can hear Him speaking under His breath. He is praying for Matthew, asking for the Lord Almighty to give him strength to face the coming storm. Asking for protection and courage.

Now He's washing my feet. I want to ask Him to stop. Does He know what's in my heart? His touch is loving, caring, and as He did with Matthew, He is praying for me. Interceding for me with the Father. Asking for strength for me. I think He's actually weeping for me as He washes my feet.

How can I betray this man? He has loved me every day. He could be the King, but is this the path to the throne—playing the part of a servant? I just don't know what to think. I wish I could stop Him. I wish I could make Him see what a mistake it is to fight against the temple power structure. If He could win them over or join them, we might have a chance to throw off Rome's tyranny.

Now He's trying to wash Peter's feet, but, to no surprise, Peter's got something to say. *"Master, you wash my feet?"*

"What I do you don't understand now, but you'll get it soon."

"You're not going to wash my feet—ever!" Peter says, standing.

"If I don't wash you, you can't be part of what I'm doing."

"Master! Not only my feet, then. Wash my hands! Wash my head!"

At this Jesus chuckles, explaining to Peter if bathed in the morning, there was no need for a bath now. Then He said:

"So now you're clean. But not every one of you."

As He says this last bit, His expression sobers. He keeps His eyes on Peter's feet, but I can feel Him reaching out to me, as though He's using everything in His Spirit to beg me not to do what I am planning.

I'll slip out as soon as He's finished with John. If I don't go soon, I'm not sure I'll have the courage. No doubt they will head from here up to the Mount of Olives. We've spent many a long night there with the Master. He loves to teach us under the stars. We'd talk about the day's events or ponder things to come. I expect they'll head up there tonight, too.

He starts to explain what He has done, but I don't hear much of what He says. My mind is going back and forth, as is my heart. One minute I want to stand with Him, the next I want to teach Him a lesson. I want to help Him see what He is getting into. As He talks on about—Wait! He just said someone will betray Him!

Next thing I know, He dips a piece of bread and hands it to me. As I eat the soggy bread, I am overcome with anger. For an instant, I hate Him. He looks me in the eye and says, "Do what you are going to do quickly."

Then I just run for it. I have no idea what the others think, but I have to get out of there. Something inside me is compelling me to this council. My mind races between visions of the money in my hand and Jesus standing before the Sanhedrin. There is one moment when, in my heart, I get a glimpse of Him—bloody and beaten and lying in the dirt—but I push it away.

This is the right thing to do. Jesus will thank me.

Is this the right thing to do?

~~~

To read the original story, see John 13.

*"If I don't wash you,
you can't be part of what I'm doing."*
John 13:8

Not Me

Peter

"You're not going to wash my feet—ever!"

I was almost shouting at Him. I could not believe Philip and Thomas let Him grovel before them like that. Doesn't He see how foolish it looks for this One who would be King to touch the filth from the streets? I said this very thing to Andrew the other day when Mary made such a scene at Simon's house.

When I began to protest, He told me I didn't understand what He was doing. I saw what He was doing; He was humiliating Himself, taking the place of a servant. I didn't want Him to touch my filthy feet. I was ashamed for Him to see what I'd been walking through, and for Him to get such filth on Himself . . . well, it would be wrong.

"Peter."

His voice broke my train of thought. I looked down into His eyes as He crouched before me.

"Master?"

"If I don't wash you, you can't be part of what I'm doing."

As He said it, He took my left foot in His hands.

I remember thinking how strong His hands were. A short three years ago, those were carpenter's hands. They were strong but gentle.

Still resisting, I quipped, "Why stop at my feet then? Wash me top to bottom—hands, head, the works!"

He chuckled and said:

"If you've had a bath in the morning, you only need your feet washed now and you're clean from head to toe. My concern, you understand, is holiness, not hygiene. So now you're clean. But not every one of you."

I watched as He finished His circuit, washing each foot, finishing with John. It was so humbling to see Him serve each of us. It reminded me of the times He would work His way through a crowd of sick and demon-possessed. He would take time with every one, sending each away not only whole, but encouraged and loved.

As He took off the soiled and soggy apron and put His tunic back on, Jesus began to talk with us.

"Do you understand what I have done to you?"

We looked around at each other, but no one was ready to speak.

"You address me as 'Teacher' and 'Master,' and rightly so. That is what I am. So if I, the Master and Teacher, washed your feet, you must now wash each other's feet. I've laid down a pattern for you. What I've done, you do. I'm only pointing out the obvious. A servant is not ranked above his master; an employee doesn't give orders to the employer. If you understand what I'm telling you, act like it—and live a blessed life.

"I'm not including all of you in this. I know precisely whom I've selected, so as not to interfere with the fulfillment of this Scripture: The one who ate bread at my table turned on his heel against me."

What was He talking about? One minute He was telling us to wash each other's feet, and the next He said we have a traitor in our midst. Sometimes I can't follow Him at all.

He continued.

"I'm telling you all this ahead of time so that when it happens you will believe that I am who I say I am. Make sure you get this right: Receiving someone I send is the same as receiving me, just as receiving me is the same as receiving the One who sent me."

Then His demeanor changed. Was He sad? Angry? He almost looked brokenhearted as He looked into our eyes.

"One of you is going to betray me."

Now we all looked around the room. Who would do such a thing? I was getting upset, but I didn't want to stick my foot in my mouth again. How could this be? We had practically lived together these last few years. How could betrayal come from within such a close community?

When I looked over at John, he was leaning back on Jesus. I nodded to him. If anyone could get away with asking a question at this point it would be John. Jesus never rebuked him.

"John," I whispered, "ask Him who."

He twisted around so He could see Jesus's face. "Lord, who is it?" Normally no one would have heard the question, but it had become so quiet in the room. I don't think any of us were even breathing.

Jesus answered with another riddle. "I will dip a morsel and give it to him."

I'm not sure what broke the tension, but we got back to eating. After a few minutes, Jesus sent Judas off to do something. I assumed he was getting things ready for the Passover tomorrow night.

Once Judas left, Jesus started teaching again. He spoke of going off someplace where we could not go. I really didn't get it. We'd been everywhere together—back and forth across the lake, up and back from Jerusalem a couple times a year. We'd all left our occupations to walk with Him day in and day out, and now He was leaving us behind?

"Where are You going, Lord?" I asked.

"You can't now follow me where I'm going. You will follow later."

That sounded foreboding, like He was headed for trouble. Whatever it was, He shouldn't face it alone. We were family now. I'd stand beside Him no matter what or who said otherwise.

"Master, why can't I follow now? I'll lay down my life for you!"

Now He looked at me, and I could almost feel His gaze. With a hint of sadness—or was it pity?—He replied:

"Really? You'll lay down your life for me? The truth is that before the rooster crows, you'll deny me three times."

He went on teaching, but I was too stunned to tune in to what He said next. He didn't trust me to stand with Him. He thought I was going to deny Him? Doesn't He know how much I love Him?

I'll show Him. I'll stand with Him. He'll see.

~~~

To read the original story, see John 13.

This cup is my blood,
my new covenant with you.
Mark 14:24

REMEMBER ME

DISCIPLE

As I stand here, unleavened bread in hand, ready to offer it to my family and friends on this Sabbath evening, I remember that night.

It was the last night; the night I thought would never end; the night I thought would end it all; the night that lasted days; the night He was betrayed.

Before all that—the betrayal, the trial, the torture, the blood—before the horrible end, we had supper. It was His last supper, I see now.

After He washed our feet, after Judas ran out—we had no idea why at the time—He took the bread. We were all talking at once. Peter and John were still trying to figure out who was going to betray Him. Thomas tried to explain to Andrew why He should never have washed their feet. Bart just talked to no one in particular about the woman with the perfume.

He stood there in silence with one piece of unleavened bread in His hands. He waited until all were quiet. He didn't interrupt us. I really think He was just enjoying the sound of our conversation. You know the sound—the sound of family, the sound of love.

We have learned so much at His side these past few years, but perhaps the most significant lesson was one of community. Many times He demanded our attention or directed our activities. Often, He taught us. But just as often, He brought us together just to be together. We'd laugh and argue and jest.

He seemed in no hurry that night. He waited. After a few minutes, the Master drew our attention as He held up the bread.

"This is My body," He said. Now there was silence. He began again. "This is My body, broken for you." As He said the word *broken,* He snapped the flatbread in half. There was something in the cracking sound that sent a chill down my spine.

I immediately thought back to that day in the wilderness when He said, "I am the bread of life." That was the day I wondered if He had lost His mind. I'll never forget His words:

"Only insofar as you eat and drink flesh and blood, the flesh and blood of the Son of Man, ... My flesh is real food and my blood is real drink. By eating my flesh and drinking my blood you enter into me and I into you."

After He had given His Father thanks for the bread, He broke it and passed it to each of us, saying:

"This is my body, broken for you. Do this to remember me."

Then He took the cup of wine and held it up. He first looked to heaven, then at each of us. He passed the cup around saying:

"This cup is my blood, my new covenant with you."

Sitting there, we had no idea that in a few short hours, His blood would be poured out, spent without reserve. But later, as I watched them whip Him with a cat-o'-nine-tails, I remembered the bread. When they pressed the crown on His head, I remembered the cup. When the nails burst through His palms and the blood flowed, I remembered the wine. When I saw them pierce His side and all that remained of His blood flowed out, I knew.

I knew He had taken the cup from the hand of the Father—the cup of wrath about which the prophet had spoken.

"This is a Message that the God of Israel gave me: 'Take this cup filled with the wine of My wrath that I'm handing to you. Make all the nations where I send you drink it down.'"

I knew He drank every drop of that wrath. This new covenant He spoke of began with Him taking the punishment for my rebellion. My sin no longer stood as a barrier between the Lord God and me. The Father, the Creator, was offering me His hand in relationship, and He paid the blood-price Himself.

So today, as we eat this bread and drink this wine, I remember.

~~~

To read the original story, see Jeremiah 25:15-16, Matthew 26:26-30, Mark 14:22-25, Luke 22:15-20, John 6:27-59, and 1 Corinthians 11:23-26.

"Don't you realize that I am able right now to call to my Father ..."
Matthew 26:53

MELEE IN THE GARDEN

MALCHUS

I want to be clear here. I am not one of His disciples.

Sure, I've heard the stories. You would have to be a hermit not to know someone He has healed, or fed, or who has been to one of His meetings. And all Jerusalem seemed to be in the temple square on the first day of the week when He rode into town, as a triumphant king would, returning victorious from some battle. Although when I saw Him on the colt, it was like inhaling peace. I don't know how to explain it, but in all the shouting and crowding and pushing, when I saw Him ... I felt shalom, the sense that everything is right and good.

Since then, the whole town has been abuzz. Messiah? Heretic? Lunatic? Who is this Jesus?

My name is Malchus, and I am a servant of Caiaphas, the high priest. It's not a bad job. The pay is good, and I get living quarters right in the center of Jerusalem. The work is not usually difficult or strenuous, but the hours can be long. It does allow me to send enough money home to support my beautiful wife and five little ones. My in-laws live with us as well, so I have many mouths to feed.

Usually my work consists of getting a scroll from the archives for the master or taking notes while he is deliberating some matter of great importance. In these last weeks, there has been much to say about Jesus. The crowds are growing with every appearance, which makes the temple priests and elders nervous. He is not making friends with the Pharisees either, which is a big mistake if you want to get anywhere in the temple system.

Thursday afternoon, one of His followers, Judas Iscariot, came to the council chamber. He entered through a side door, and Caiaphas almost had me escort him out. But then he said he had information about Jesus and knew how we could take Him quietly.

This got the council's interest. They had been looking for opportunities to take Him since before I came to work for the high priest a year ago, but there are always crowds. The council does not want to cause a riot. They just want to pull Jesus aside, out of the public eye, and see if they can get Him to ease up on all this rhetoric. They have seen it before, and Caiaphas knows firsthand how crowds become mobs at the drop of a coin. They need this Jesus to back off a bit and, at the very least, consider keeping it outside the city limits.

In any case, they've been looking for a less public way to take Jesus. This Judas said he could bring us right to Jesus, and we would only have to deal with His little troupe of characters.

Judas said he would lead us right to Jesus that very night for thirty pieces of silver. He said Jesus frequently went off to pray, and he knew the place.

"Those boys don't know how to fight, so you shouldn't need a lot of men, and I have never seen Jesus's hands do anything but good. Now promise me you're not going to do Him any harm. His intentions are good, but He's getting carried away. You're just going to talk to Him, ask Him to get control of the crowds, right?"

"Here's your silver; now be on your way. We will be ready when you come."

As soon as Judas left, Annas, Caiaphas's father-in-law and one of his chief advisors, suggested we pressure the Romans to send a cohort for the mission. What we needed with six hundred men, I had no idea. From what I'd seen, this man was no threat.

Then Caiaphas called me over and directed me to go with them that night to witness the event.

As the afternoon passed and we prepared for the evening's raid, I remembered the address Caiaphas had made a few weeks back. It was on the temple steps during his Purim address, in which he spoke of the death of Haman. He said it was "expedient for one man to die on behalf of the people." I began to wonder if this was all going to end badly.

The council sent me down to speak to Pilate, the Roman Prefect over all Judea, which Rome now considered hers. Caiaphas demanded that if Pilate did not want a real mob scene, we would need his help to silence this Jesus. It would be in Pilate's best interest to assist in the capture of this man.

After a bit of back and forth, Pilate agreed to send a cohort, but he would not release them until the traitor was ready to go. He ordered that no one was to leave the barracks that evening, and they would assemble once Judas had returned. He wanted to see if this spy would be back or if he would take the money and run.

The evening dragged on and on. I was supposed to have been at home with my family on this night of preparation. Passover was close at hand, and the festivities had begun in earnest.

It was nearly the third watch of the night before Judas showed up to let us know Jesus was heading to His secret place. I headed over to the Roman consulate to notify the head of the guards that the time had come.

Now he had to get the army assembled and ready to move. Many of the men had seen Jesus here and there, and the whole group was halfhearted about this mission.

After what seemed like hours, we were ready to move. Every sixth man carried a torch, and each man carried sword and shield. I remember thinking again about the absurdity of going after this man with an army— this man who never attempts to conceal Himself. It seemed absurd to me.

I found myself out in front as Judas and I led the procession. The two of us didn't fit with either the military unit or the chief priests and officers of the temple and elders. He seemed nervous, or perhaps he was second-guessing himself. When he saw the army we led, he almost gave up the whole thing. I think he was beginning realize that we weren't just bringing Jesus in for questioning.

He led us to an olive grove called the garden of Gethsemane. As we drew near, I noticed people milling about, some with torches. We stopped a little way back, and the traitor went ahead of us. He kissed one of the men on the cheek. It was our signal—this was the man.

This is where it all gets a little fuzzy in my mind. Everything happened in quick sequence. As we approached the clearing, the man Judas had kissed, Jesus Himself, came toward us to head us off and keep us from the others.

"Who are you after?" came a voice from the predawn mist.

"Jesus the Nazarene." The centurion who acted as head of the cohort replied on our behalf.

Jesus spoke again, and the strangest thing happened. I heard Him say "I AM," and all six hundred of the soldiers and the rest of us fell to the ground. What a clatter in the still of the morning in that deserted place! It was like the first clap of thunder preceding a midsummer night's storm.

Until that moment, we all thought the evening was going to be a waste of time. Now every nerve was twitching, and as we all regained our footing, the soldiers put hand to sword.

As I got to my feet, I heard Jesus ask again:

"Who are you after?"

Again, the reply came from the head of the Romans. *"Jesus the Nazarene."*

"I told you," said Jesus, *"that's me. I'm the one. So if it's me you're after, let these others go."*

From the corner of my eye, I noticed one of Jesus's men searching around for something. It was hard to see in the mist and torchlight, but I realized he had a sword in his hand. He was flailing it about as though he had not held a weapon in decades.

The uneasy feeling in my gut was soon justified as he headed right for me, ready to chop off my head. As I dove to the ground again, I felt cool steel on my cheek and then the warmth of blood running down my face and soaking my tunic.

I thought I should be in pain and wondered if I was even alive. I was afraid, angry, confused. As I put my hand to the side of my head to stop the bleeding and assess the damage, I realized the ear was gone. My ear was gone! And then the pain overwhelmed me.

At the same time, the Roman soldiers drew their weapons, and it looked like a full-blown melee was about to ensue. Then Jesus simply put up His hand.

"Stop! No more of this," He said.

Before I knew it, Jesus was standing right in front of me. He got down on one knee and helped me to a sitting position. He pulled my hand away from the side of my head and placed my ear right where it belonged. I have no idea how He managed to find it in the dust and predawn murkiness. Then He helped me to my feet.

The pain was gone, and I could hear. I couldn't be sure, but I thought I was hearing better than I had been earlier in the day. I was stunned.

I didn't know what to do. Should I thank Him? Should I arrest Him? Should I worship Him? Who is this man?

Then He spoke again.

"Put your sword back where it belongs. All who use swords are destroyed by swords. Don't you realize that I am able right now to call to my Father, and twelve companies—more, if I want them—of fighting angels would be here, battle-ready? But if I did that, how would the Scriptures come true that say this is the way it has to be?"

As this man who sliced off my ear skulked back to the other disciples, he mumbled something about Jesus telling him to bring the sword in the first place.

Again Jesus spoke, this time addressing the chief priests and officers of the temple and elders who had come to arrest Him.

"What is this, jumping me with swords and clubs as if I were a dangerous criminal? Day after day I've been with you in the Temple and you've not so much as lifted a hand against me. But do it your way—it's a dark night, a dark hour."

At that point, His band disappeared into the grove, and Jesus gave Himself into our custody.

They all headed back into the city, but I lagged behind. I could take no further role in this drama. It was all wrong. Who is this man that by simple words can decimate an army in one breath and calm it with the next? Who can pick up a detached ear and replace it with hardly a thought? Who is this man?

~~~

To read the original story, see Matthew 26:45-57, Mark 14:43-50, Luke 22:47-54, and John 18:1-12.

"Don't get mixed up in judging this noble man.
I've just been through a long and troubled night
because of a dream about him."
Matthew 27:19

NIGHTMARES

PILATE'S WIFE

It's been thirty-eight hours since I really slept. I suppose I was asleep when the dream started, but I can't count that.

While I was cleaning up after dinner last night, they came and took my husband. It was those Jews. They don't care in the least that people have schedules; people have lives.

My husband has the seemingly impossible job of keeping the peace between Romans like us and the Jews in this godforsaken dust bowl of a city. They still pretend to own this city and the land, yet it is Rome's flag flying here in Jerusalem. It's Roman coin that buys their bread and meat.

And apparently it was Roman justice they sought last night.

What was so urgent that they had to call my husband away on a fifth night of the week? Surely it could wait till next week, whatever it was. At least that is what I was thinking when they interrupted our evening yesterday.

I waited a few hours, but finally dozed off right in my chair.

Then the dreams started. First I saw my husband, Pilate. The Jewish mob spat on him from every side. Then they slapped his face. Then they tore his robes off and threw him to the ground. But as he writhed in pain from the beating he endured, I saw his face. It wasn't Pilate. It was Jesus, the one they brought to our door last night.

When I saw His face it woke me.

After a few more minutes, I began to doze again. Again it was my husband, this time in his full uniform. There was no question; it was Pilate. I always thought he looked so handsome in his full-dress uniform with plumes and bars, brass and iron.

As I looked on, the Jewish high priest yanked off Pilate's helmet and pressed a wreath into his brow—like one a winning athlete might wear, only this one was made of thorns. As the blood streamed down his cheeks, again I saw His face—Jesus's—on my husband's body.

I was awake again, and now I did not want to sleep anymore.

I got up and started walking. I got some figs. I thought if I could keep eating, I would not sleep, but after an hour, my eyelids again closed. Immediately I saw my husband, only this time he was completely naked! As I watched, his own soldiers forced him to pick up a cross that lay on the ground before him. As he bent to pick it up, I heard a whip crack and his body collapsed. When he finally got the cross up on his back and stood

. . . it was me! The horrible cross crushed me, and as I collapsed under its weight, my face became His, the Jewish magician, Jesus.

Every time I closed my eyes, I saw Him take the torture away from me—away from my husband—and take it upon Himself.

I pulled on my robe and ran all the way to the chamber where my husband governs and meets to settle grievances.

They were all there. I didn't know any of them, and yet they had all been in my dreams—the high priest, the soldiers, and Jesus Himself. As I approached the hall, I could hear echoes of anger in their voices.

When they realized I had entered, everyone got quiet. The high priest stopped the shouting I could hear moments before and glared at me in angry silence. This was the man who pressed the thorns into my husband's brow—into Jesus's brow—in my dream.

I went right over to my husband. I could see this angered him.

"What are you doing?" His tone stung and his word carried not the slightest nod toward civility.

"Don't get mixed up in judging this noble man. I've just been through a long and troubled night because of a dream about him."

"I can't let a man go because you had a bad dream," he said, mocking me.

I was certain every hurt he inflicted on this just man would come back to haunt him for the rest of his life.

"Listen to me!" I said. But there was a tinge of panic in my voice, and this undermined my credibility with him.

"Get out! You don't belong here, and you cannot tell me what to do because of your *dream*." He was furious because I had made a spectacle in front of these Jews.

Now I am afraid to sleep.

I wish there was something I could do to stop this, but he won't even listen to me now. I'm afraid they're going to crucify this Jesus, and I'm sure it's a huge mistake.

~~~

To read the original story, see Matthew 27:19.

"I've found nothing in him deserving death.
I'm going to warn him to watch his step and let him go."
Luke 23:22

BLOODY HANDS

PILATE

Will this day ever end? Every time I go to the window, I am sick to my stomach. Part of me wants to run all the way to the hill and stop it, to make them take Him down.

Usually I attend such crucifixions in person. It enforces our authority over these people. It lets them know we aren't afraid to act. But this is not right.

I don't want to be part of the mob watching Him die. It's grown strangely dark since they lifted Him up, and yet somehow I can still see it through the window. This darkness doesn't feel right. It doesn't seem like weather. The air itself seems to be furious, like the gods are getting ready to pour out their anger toward all mankind.

I look down at my hands, the hands I washed in front of the mob to show them I was not taking responsibility for this man's blood. "Let His blood be on us and on our children!" the people cried. Though washed, there is still blood on my hands. An innocent man hangs there on that tree, and His blood is on me.

What was His crime? He's accused of blasphemy. What is that to me? I am no Jew. He wasn't trying to rule me. He was no threat to Caesar; His own people wouldn't follow Him. There was not one to take His part, to stand beside Him, to testify for Him. He stood alone. Not much of an insurrection.

He did seem to be in control, though. No matter what I said, He wasn't fazed. He didn't flinch when I said I had the power to take His life. In fact, He looked me straight in the eye and told me my power came from His Father. My informers told me His father was a carpenter from Galilee, and he had been dead for years.

Was this man a pathological liar? Why bring His dead father into the conversation at all? Anyone else would have declared their innocence or denied the charges. A liar would have backed away from the accusations. He just stood there in silence. He was no liar.

He didn't seem to be afraid either. Perhaps He was just a lunatic. Perhaps He didn't understand the charges against Him. But I didn't understand the charges against Him either. Why should it bother me so to be rid of a man who was not in His right mind? You would have to be crazy to be so calm in the face of the anger and hate I witnessed today. No. I looked into His eyes. He was no lunatic.

He would not speak before the crowd, but when I put the question to Him, when I asked Him if He was the King of the Jews, what did He say?

"If you say so."

Was He asking me to decide if He was a king? Was He asking me to be His subject, to give my life over to His kingship?

Three times I refused those Jews. Three times I took Him back out and tried to release Him. Three times they refused me. Three times they demanded His blood.

Why does this bother me so?

Why is my heart in such turmoil?

Why can't I get this blood off my hands?

~~~

To read the original story, see Matthew 27, Mark 15, Luke 23, and John 18-19.

> He had wanted for a long time to see him,
> he'd heard so much about him.
> He hoped to see him do something spectacular.
> Luke 23:8

HEROD'S TRAVESTY

HEROD'S CUPBEARER

Yes, I was there the night Jesus came before Herod.

I serve as Herod's cupbearer, so I've seen a lot. Usually we hold court up north in Galilee, but during the feasts, Herod likes to come down and be in the center of the action here in Jerusalem.

I have been with Herod for a dozen years. I took the position after my father died. He served as cupbearer for Herod the Great until his death thirty years back. It was not long after the massacre— when Herod the Great ordered the killing of every boy two years old or younger. I was not young enough to be in danger, but we all knew victim families. I can remember my father weeping with his brother who lost his only son in that holocaust.

I must be ever so careful in my job. I am convinced that Herod Antipas, my master, is almost as mad as his father. This is a cruel and ambitious family.

Herod is acutely aware of any threat that might arise and upset the peace in Galilee or Perea. He tries to keep an eye on the latest news and gossip about this prophet from Galilee.

About a year and a half ago, Herod began to fret over the ministry of this prophet. It was when he heard Jesus was sending out His followers to preach and perform miracles. He sensed this roaming holy man might become a threat to his own rule.

Someone spread a rumor in the court, suggesting Jesus was the reincarnation of John the Baptist, and it really set Herod off. He had been afraid of John. He'd not been the same since the day he called for John's head. It haunted him.

So when he heard John was back from the dead and doing miracles, it unnerved him.

Since then, he demands daily reports about the activities of Jesus. He has spies following Him everywhere—some posing as disciples, others as hecklers.

That's why he jumped at the chance to interrogate Jesus himself. As with John, he fears this man, but at the same time he wants to see a miracle with his own eyes. Every time one of his spies comes and tells us of a miracle, Herod extracts every detail. Then he tries to come up with a natural explanation for each account.

When Jesus arrived in our court, He was a mess. The Romans had not treated Him well. They delivered Him to us with a band of high-ranking Jewish leaders. The chief priests and scribes came along to make their accusations.

Herod took one look at Jesus in His tattered robes and mocked Him openly. This started a chain reaction, and soon everyone in the court began to jest and insult Him. One of the soldiers grabbed Him by the beard and yanked out a handful of whiskers. Some spat in His face; others hurled vile words.

As the Jews accused Him and Herod taunted Him, Jesus stood in silence. Silence.

Herod tried everything: sweetness, rudeness, insults, bribes— anything to get a rise out of Jesus. He had his attendants strip off His filthy garments and dress Him in one of Herod's royal robes. It looked ridiculous. Herod was easily twice His size.

Though Herod mocked, the Jewish leaders who came along could not have been more serious. They became more passionate with every accusation they spouted. I thought the chief priest was going to have a stroke.

What was it about this Jesus that got everyone so riled up? He was the eye of a great storm, completely still and calm while waves crashed on every side.

Herod grew tired of it all when it became apparent he held no power over Him. So, like a horse by its reins, they drew Jesus back across Jerusalem to Pilate's palace.

Herod's mood was foul that night, but he did have one of his scribes write a note thanking Pilate for sending Jesus his way. They had never been friendly, but this act by Pilate seemed to break the ice. Perhaps they felt some kind of shared guilt in the death of this good man.

~~~

To read the original story, see Luke 23:6-12.

As they led him off, they made Simon, a man from Cyrene
who happened to be coming in from the countryside,
carry the cross behind Jesus.
Luke 23:26

WATCH YOUR BROTHER

RUFUS, SON OF SIMON OF CYRENE

My papa tells me I'm almost a man. That day, I had to be strong; I had to be the man for my little brother. I know he was afraid, because I could taste my own fear. If it wasn't for the rope Papa tied around our waists to keep us together, I'm sure I would have lost little Alex.

The soldiers grabbed Papa just after we got into the city. We live in the countryside, about a two-day's walk from Jerusalem. My mother was from Egypt, so my papa moved there when they married. He came from Cyrene, far to the west of here.

I've been coming to Jerusalem with my papa for as long as I can remember, because there is a synagogue for Cyrenians here. The first time we made the trip together was the year my mother was pregnant with my little brother, Alex. I guess I was two at the time.

When we got into the city this morning, something seemed to be wrong. It's always crowded when we're here, because we only come during the holy days to offer our lamb for the Passover. But the crowds were gathering outside the city this time. You couldn't get onto the road, and the people were just standing all along the side.

At first I thought it might be a parade. Sometimes the Romans like to march their armies through the streets. Papa says they want everyone to know how strong they are. But this procession was headed away from the city.

When we got close enough to hear what was going on, the crowd seemed angry. They were yelling out curses at the procession. I know some of those words, but I'm not allowed to say them. I caught a glimpse of a man carrying a cross through the dust, and then my papa told us what was going on.

"They're punishing criminals," he said. "They put them up on those crossed beams and make them die there. It's horrible!"

I spied a gap in the crowd and ran up so I could see what was happening. Alex didn't want to look, so he covered his eyes while I pulled him along by the rope around our waists.

Just as we got to the spot where the crowds thinned, another criminal walked by. He fell to the ground right in front of me, almost crushed by the weight of the cross. This man was covered in blood, and there was some kind of wreath on His head. Where the long thorns of the wreath dug into His brow, blood ran down from each needle and streaked His face. His hair and beard were matted with it. His ragged clothes were bloody too. The dirt from the road clung to everything and mixed with the blood to form a purple mess.

That's when they grabbed my father. Two Roman soldiers grabbed him by the arms and pulled him out of the crowd. As they took him, he turned to me and told me to hold onto my brother. They made Papa lift the cross off the bloody man's back. Then they forced Him up too. They pushed Him along in front of my father.

As the procession started to move, Papa looked back at me and called out, "You're the man now! Don't lose Alexander."

I looked at Alex. He was crying. I took his hand and put it on the rope. "Come on, Alex, we have to keep up."

I pulled him into the street, and we followed my father. In front of him was the man with the crown of thorns. He could barely walk. I've never seen so much blood. He kept stumbling to the ground.

After the third time He fell, they made my papa put his arm around this "king" and practically carry Him. It was all Papa could do to carry the weight of the cross and the remains of this man he hefted with his arm.

By the time they got to the place of the skull, the captive's blood covered my father. We were not far behind them. At the crest of the hill, they took the cross from Papa and dropped it on the ground. It almost hurt me to watch the way they handled the prisoner.

Two guards grabbed Him under His arms and dragged Him onto the beam. His blood-soaked back dragged across that rough-hewn post. Once they had Him where they wanted Him, they pulled out some huge spikes.

My papa found us and made us turn away. I kept trying to look. I'm not sure what was drawing me, but I could not turn away on my own. My father pulled us away from the bloody scene, and we headed up to the Cyrenian synagogue.

We were not all right. My little brother was shaking, and I couldn't sleep for the next couple nights.

In fact, I didn't get a good night's sleep again until the first day of the week. That's when we heard this Jesus, this one they called the King of the Jews, was alive.

My papa said he thinks Jesus is Messiah, the One we have been waiting for.

~~~

To read the original story, see Matthew 27:32, Mark 15:21, and Luke 23:26.

"Father, I place my life in your hands!"
Luke 23:46

THIS WAS THE SON OF GOD

CENTURION

If I have seen one criminal die, I have seen a hundred. I am tasked with ensuring they are dead before we end these torturous crucifixions.

Sometimes we leave these worthless men hanging for days, but at times like this, with the Jew's Holy days coming, Pilate has us rush things a bit. Once he feels they have been sufficiently crushed and humiliated, he will have us break their legs. When it comes to that, these hardened criminals nearly beg for the relief they think death will bring. Breaking their legs brings death in minutes.

But today . . . well, I've never seen anything like this before.

There were three trees planted on the hill today, three men facing the price for their crimes against Rome. Left and right were thieves—repeat offenders. Roman law is stern. The more public and harsh the punishment, the more cowed the populous. You don't need to see many crucifixions to decide to give up a life of crime.

But this One in the center . . . I mean, I've seen criminals talk from the cross before, but it's always been either a plea for mercy, cries of innocence, or, more often than not, it's bitter and foul refuse flying from their mouths. But His words . . . Even on the cross there was life in them.

Rather than being consumed by His own pain and agony, He looked down and gave the care of His mother to another man. He even seemed to be comforting one of the other criminals while they both struggled for breath.

He didn't blame, beg, or curse. He forgave. Forgave! Who does that?

"Father, forgive them; they don't know what they're doing."

There was a moment when His agony peaked, but it did not seem related to the pain He was bearing. He cried out:

"My God, my God, why have you abandoned me?"

116

If it were possible, it seemed to grow even darker at that moment. Then I felt the rumble; thunder, I thought.

The end is usually ugly, but not for this man.

It was almost like He decided it was time to die and just passed on. When the Jews accused Him and Rome put Him on this cross, they intended to take His life from Him. But when He was ready, He said, "It is finished. Father, take my Spirit. I trust you with it." And then His breathing stopped. Man intended to take His life, but in the end He gave it up Himself.

That's when things got really strange.

The rumble returned. The sky was so dark it would be no surprise to hear such a roar from above. But as the rumble grew, things started shaking. It seemed the ground was about to open up and swallow us all!

The earth itself was breaking apart as this Son of glory and sorrow breathed His last.

A breach opened up clear across the city—through the temple and into the graveyard. What a mess! There have been stories of dead men walking the streets. The Jews are in full-blown panic because the breach has compromised their most holy place.

Are these raindrops the tears of a brokenhearted God pouring down to wash away the blood of a millennium of sacrifices?

Truly this was the Son of God.

~~~

To read the original story, see Matthew 27, Mark 15, Luke 23, and John 19.

At that moment, the Temple curtain
was ripped in two, top to bottom.
Matthew 27:51

A TORN VEIL
TEMPLE PRIEST

Darkness ruled the day. Yes, it was dark outside, but it's also dark inside. The only light in the holy place is from a golden lampstand. Its seven lights burn day and night to illuminate this place.

I came into the Lord's house to add oil to the lamp. I'm a priest of the Lord Almighty, and we're tasked with caring for this holy place. I have never had the privilege of going beyond the veil to the Holy of Holies, but I often come in here to clean, add oil to the lampstand, or refresh the laver in the outer court.

Most of the other priests headed over to Golgotha that day. There was another crucifixion. For the most part, we priests stay away from such gruesome events. Rome can be so cruel. I have never witnessed one, but I know some priests have had to declare themselves unclean for seven days, just because of all the blood.

But this crucifixion has drawn out most of the priesthood. Even Caiaphas and Annas were there. I'm not sure what would happen if they're rendered unclean. I would end up doing all the work in here for the Passover week if that were to happen.

As I filled the oil reservoir in the seven-headed lampstand, I felt the rumble. At first I assumed it was finally going to rain, and I expected to see the flash of lightning. Then the shaking began. This was no small tremor. I heard a crash and the splashing of water as the laver in the outer court toppled to the ground. Then the table of shewbread tumbled over.

It was then I noticed the crack in the floor. I held on to the lampstand as much to steady myself as to keep it from falling. The crack ran right up the center of the holy place and headed for the veil separating me from the Holy of Holies.

This thirty-foot-high, six-foot-thick curtain began to flap wildly. I moved to the wall behind me to get out of its reach. I heard the Ark of the

Covenant banging around behind the curtain, and then it split. The veil of the temple tore right down the middle, from top to bottom.

I covered my eyes. I was afraid for my life. No priest could go into that place without weeks of preparation. You would never approach the mercy seat without a cord around your ankle.

Then, as abruptly as it started, the shaking stopped. I was still holding the lamp, and it was still burning. By its dim light, I detected a gap in the entrance to the Holy of Holies. It was no longer a solid curtain. There was a breach; it was one man wide.

Had the Almighty Himself stepped down from that mercy seat, thrust the curtains aside, and walked out of that most holy place?

For centuries, we've known exactly where to find God: in the Ark beyond the veil. But now God is no longer behind the veil, no longer in a box. God is among His people.

~~~

To read the original story, see Matthew 27:51, and Mark 15:38.

...tombs were opened up,
and many bodies of believers asleep
in their graves were raised.
Matthew 27:52

FIRSTFRUITS

CITIZEN OF JERUSALEM

Today is the day we normally celebrate the Firstfruits—the first day of the week after the Passover celebration. It's the day we offer to the Lord the first portion of our first harvest. It's a day of thanksgiving and faith.

We thank Him for His provision of soil, sun, and rain. For the gift of a fruitful field. And we pray His blessings over the coming harvest.

Usually it's one of the most festive times of the year for us. As Jews living in Jerusalem, we host the celebration of our greatest holy day. Relatives from all over Palestine make their annual pilgrimage to offer sacrifice here in this most holy city.

We eat and drink and remember. It's a time of joy and laughter. We remember those who have gone before us into the arms of Father Abraham and we cry. We remember the Passover when the Lord delivered us out of the cruel hands of Egypt.

This year things were more subdued. After the earthquake on Friday night devastated the temple, the priests scrambled to find a way to offer the Passover sacrifices to the Lord.

The sight of this young prophet Jesus on the cross shocked many of us. I had hoped He might be the Messiah, the One I've awaited all my life. He had captured my imagination with His teachings and the miracles He performed. But now He is dead, and the city seems to be mourning.

Less than a week ago I heard Him teaching in Bethany, where they say He raised Lazarus from the dead. One thing He said really stuck with me:

"Unless a grain of wheat is buried in the ground, dead to the world, it is never any more than a grain of wheat. But if it is buried, it sprouts and reproduces itself many times over."

This morning the strangest thing happened. As I headed for the temple to see what was going on for today's Firstfruit offerings, I saw a man who looked exactly like my uncle Eli. Exactly! He walked by me as though he did not recognize me. It's no wonder; my uncle Eli died when I was eight.

There were others, many others, walking the streets of Jerusalem dressed in out-of-date clothes.

They all seemed to be heading for the temple.

Then two men came running across the street. They ran away from the center of town at full speed. I recognized one of them as Peter. He was one of Jesus's men from Galilee.

Why would they still be here in Jerusalem now that their leader is dead? Where were they off to in such a hurry?

I really don't know what to expect today. These are strange days. It's almost like they planted Jesus as a seed, and the dead are sprouting up on this day of Firstfuits.

What strange days are upon us!

~~~

To read the original story, see Matthew 27:52-53.

RESURRECTION

Jesus said, "Mary."
John 20:16

MY WEEPING IS OVER

I tell you, I've seen Him with my own eyes! I didn't dream this whole thing up.

Here's what happened.

Friday, just before the Sabbath, Joseph managed to get us the body before sundown. I think he spoke directly to Pilate. From what he told me, Pilate was glad to have Him off that cruel cross.

I had no idea what to do. I'd never buried a man before, but I knew we couldn't leave Him out there. Thank the Lord for Joseph. He gave us his own tomb. It was a cave in the side of a hill not far from Golgotha, near the resting place of his ancestors. I remember how Jesus had called us all sisters and brothers, those of us who followed Him. I'm sorry, I'm babbling. Where was I?

Friday night we put Him in the tomb, but we didn't have time to do it well. I wanted to adorn the horrid place so it looked like something other than just a hole in a rock. I wanted to wrap Him up. To be honest, I just wanted to see Him once more.

The sun was not up when I left the house. When I got to His grave, the predawn mist swirling about, I saw guards sitting beside the massive stone blocking the entrance to the tomb. The sight of it broke my heart afresh, and I began to weep again. I collapsed to the ground and buried my face in my apron.

It was then I felt the earth begin to shake. Another earthquake? As the earth stopped its rumble, I heard a commotion near the tomb. I looked up, and where the guards had been just moments before, there were two beings. Their brightness was greater than the brilliant sun which had just peeked over the eastern horizon. Not only that—the tomb was open. Someone had moved the boulder away from the mouth of the tomb.

I flashed back to last week when Jesus called Lazarus out of his burial cave. It took three men to move that stone, and it was much smaller than this one.

I ran to the mouth of the cave, tears still pouring down my face. The man on the right—an angel, I suppose—said to me:

"Woman, why do you weep?"

I could see the cave was empty. My mind was racing. Where were the guards? Had they moved the stone and taken the Lord with them? Where could they have gone? What was going on?

My sorrow now mixed with anger, fear, and confusion. I looked down at my hands; I still carried the fragrances I intended to use in the tomb. I held them up and somehow managed to speak.

"They took my Master," I said, *"and I don't know where they put him."*

What was I going to do now?

I turned away from the tomb, head to the ground. Things kept getting worse. First they killed this wonderful man, and then they stole His body. Why? The tears just kept coming.

As I moved away from the tomb, I saw feet before me and heard a voice.

"Woman, why do you weep? Who are you looking for?" He said.

Why is this gardener talking to me? Can't he see I just want to grieve? There was a hint of anger in my voice when I replied.

"Mister, if you took him, tell me where you put him so I can care for him."

Even as I said it, I was replaying His voice in my mind. I knew that voice.

Then He said my name.

"Mary."

At that instant, the moment I heard Him say my name, it all left—the sorrow, the anger, the fear, the confusion. It rolled away, like the stone before His tomb. And like the death that tried to take Him away, these no longer had a hold on me.

"Rabboni!"

I fell to my knees before Him and reached for His feet. I could see the nail holes in those beautiful feet. As I reached for Him, He said:

"Don't cling to me, for I have not yet ascended to the Father. Go to my brothers and tell them, 'I ascend to my Father and your Father, my God and your God.'"

I didn't know what to say or do. I knew only this: He was alive!

I heard something behind me, and as I turned to see what was rustling, He vanished. Was I imagining it? Did I dream it? There is no way this was my imagination. The tomb was empty; and He had risen.

I headed back into town to tell the disciples. When I got there, the mood was the same as it had been for three days. Most of them were still in shock. I burst through the door and cried out to them, "He's alive! He's alive! He is alive!" Then I told them all about it. Before I finished telling my story, Peter and John were on their way.

It's only been three days since the worst day I ever imagined. The glory of this new day—this first day—swallowed up all the horror and turned it into something beautiful, something wonderful. He is risen!

~~~

To read the original story, see Matthew 28:1-11, Mark 16:9-10, and John 20:11-18.

"So, you believe because
you've seen with your own eyes."
John 20:29

I Believe

Thomas

The night He was betrayed, I ran. We all scattered, but I ran. Left town.

We were all in the garden praying together after dinner. That's not entirely true. He was praying; the rest of us were sleeping. Then a mob arrived and surrounded us, soldiers and temple guards. Peter started to fight, but the Master told him to put up his sword. The whole night has become a blur in my memory. Jesus spoke to their leader and then motioned for us to leave Him.

It's strange how fear can completely undo hope. My expectation was gone. My hope that by next year at the Passover Jesus would be ruling as King left me. My anticipation of freedom from this Roman tyranny fled that very night.

When I was still young, my brother and I watched as Roman soldiers dragged my father off to prison. He had a rebellious streak, I guess, and would often push them with his taunting. I never saw him again. My mother, for fear we would see the same fate, never even let us raise our eyes around the Romans.

So when I saw the trouble Jesus was in with Rome, all hope left me.

I think John and Peter hid and then followed the procession back to the city, but I ran for it. I admit it. I was afraid.

I ran back to the home where we spent the last week and gathered my things, and by the time the sun reached its apex, I was well on my way to Emmaus. I have family there, and I knew they would keep me safe.

That's where I was when I heard He was dead. It broke my heart. The guilt came like waves, over and over. I know I could not have freed Him. But after the way He loved us while we walked together, to just run away was . . . well, I felt like a coward, a traitor. The very night He called me friend, I turned and ran.

Then on the first day of the week, I began hearing rumors that He was not dead. First I heard they killed the wrong man. Then I heard they botched the crucifixion. I didn't know what to believe, so I stirred up what courage I could and headed back to Jerusalem. It was the second day of the week when I arrived back in town.

When I got there, I found the doors locked. I could hear the buzz of conversation inside, and I recognized Peter's distinctive voice. I knocked and called to them.

"Let me in! It's me. Thomas."

Once inside, I picked up on the discussion.

"Do you think He'll show up today?"

"Should we go look for Him?"

"He knows where to find us."

I wasn't sure what to make of it, so I grabbed Andrew and asked what was going on.

"He's alive! Jesus has risen from the dead! He was here last night."

"Last night?" I said. "Are you sure it was Him? Did He really die?"

Hearing my questions, John came over to me.

"I watched Him die. I saw the whole thing from start to finish. I watched—stood by, helpless—as they scourged Him. I felt the pounding of the cruel sledge as it fastened Him to the beam. I even saw them drive a spear in Him, and I fell into the mud as the blood and water poured from His side. He was dead.

"I helped Joseph wrap His body for burial. He was cold. Dead. Jesus was no longer in that body.

"Then on the first day of the week, while we were hiding here, Mary burst through the doors. She was crying and laughing and trying to tell us something. She was saying the tomb was empty, and she had seen Him in the garden outside the cave where we'd put His body.

"By the time I understood what she was trying to tell us, Peter was already gone—running toward the grave. I took off after him. When I arrived at the tomb, I stuck my head inside. Sure enough, it was empty.

Peter, still running at full tilt, ran right past me and didn't stop till he was in the cave.

"But that's not the best part. We came back here to tell the others. Mary kept claiming to have seen Him, but the others were skeptical. As we threw ideas back and forth, He just appeared in the center of the room! We had the doors locked against the authorities, but there He stood, holding out His hands to us. You know the way He used to gesture to the crowds with that 'come unto Me' look? But this time there were gaping holes in His palms. He pulled back His robes and showed us the gash the spear made.

"He was here, Thomas, right in this room."

I can't believe it—won't believe it—until I see Him with my own eyes. I told John I would have to see it myself before I even began to hope.

Days passed and still I doubted. Though all the others had verified what John said, I could not accept it. I guess the mess in the garden with swords and Jewish authorities and Romans had unnerved me.

One night, after almost a week hunkered down with the others in the home on the outskirts of the city, He came. We were all there, the eleven of us and the women, all locked in tight.

With no warning at all, He was just there! Right in the center of the room. In fact, as I think about it, I realize He was closest to me, right behind me. As I turned to see what was going on, He spoke:

"Peace to you."

Then He said to me:

"Take your finger and examine my hands. Take your hand and stick it in my side. Don't be unbelieving. Believe."

Stunned, I fell to my knees.

"My Master! My God!"

Then Jesus looked around at all of us and said:

"So, you believe because you've seen with your own eyes. Even better blessings are in store for those who believe without seeing."

Doubt and fear left me for the last time. I didn't need to touch Him. I didn't even need to see Him. When I heard His voice, I believed. Down to the core of my being, I believed.

~~~

To read the original story, see John 20:24-31.

"Simon, son of John, do you love me?"
John 21:17

I'm Going Fishing

PETER

It's been a couple weeks since we found the empty tomb, and things are just not getting back to normal. After the first night when Jesus appeared in our midst, James and John started talking about heading back to Jerusalem. They wanted to put Jesus on a warhorse instead of a donkey this time and march into the city. What could stop Jesus from taking His rightful place in the temple—or in the palace, for that matter?

But then a few days passed. Thomas returned and we were unable to convince him that Jesus had risen from the dead. We hadn't seen Him in days. We got together every day in the same room where He had appeared to us that first night. At first we'd met there to avoid capture by the Jewish leadership. After watching the way they got rid of Jesus, we were afraid for our lives.

Since His first appearance, we met there every day, always expecting Jesus to show up again. I wasn't sure everyone would be back after the Sabbath, but we all knew what we saw. We hoped He would join us again.

Finally, after eight long days, Jesus appeared again, and this time Thomas was with us. Jesus offered his hands and His side to Thomas. But again, no word about what was next.

Of course Jesus never gave us much warning about what was coming. It always seemed like He knew just what to do and when, but we never had the week's itinerary beforehand. We'd get up in the morning, and Jesus would tell us to go to Samaria or lead us over to Cana. Sometimes He just told us, "Head across the lake; I will catch up with you in Capernaum."

In the last three years, I can't remember a stretch of eight days when we weren't off doing something.

But now, silence.

Yesterday morning I was pretty frustrated as we sat and waited. It was past midday, and I had to do something.

"I'm going fishing," I said

Half the guys followed me out the door. We left the rest of them there waiting, but I could not stand another day of doing nothing.

Fishing has always been what I turn to when I don't know what else to do. It's been like home to me since I was a boy. I used to go out with James and John on their father's boat. There's so much there that's familiar. It lets my mind work out problems. It's where I screwed up enough courage to ask for my wife's hand in marriage. It's where I learned to pray. It's where I met Him, on the shores of the lake.

The others who came along did so not because they loved the idea. It was more likely they, like me, just didn't know what else to do.

It was a long night, and it wasn't helping. Usually out on the water in the calm of the night, under a patchwork of stars and clouds, my mind and heart opened up. But this night it was shut up tight. Something was weighing on me. I'm not even sure what it was, but there was a pressure building inside me.

Besides all that, the fishing was unproductive—every net, every cast, empty. Even Andrew, who loves to drop a line off the back of the boat while we work the nets, came up with nothing.

It reminded me of the first time I met Him. We had been out all night and caught nothing, just like tonight. As we sat cleaning our nets, He walked up with a huge crowd of folks pressing in on Him. He walked right up to me and asked if I would take Him just offshore so everyone could hear and see Him.

The crowd spread out on the hillside, and we put out a couple dozen cubits. Then He taught them. At first I kept busy with the cleaning of our nets, so they would be ready for the next day, but as He spoke, His words drew me. They had a force, a pull I couldn't resist. I noticed James and John sat listening on the shore, nets in their laps.

I have no idea how long He spoke, but after a bit, He turned to me and said,

"Let's go get some fish. Take us out a ways, will you?"

I remember thinking, "This young zealot may know everything about God, but He doesn't know much about fishing. If there were going to be fish, they would have been there last night. Now it's the heat of the day, and we won't be seeing any fish till evening."

Still, I was so impressed with His speaking that I jumped at the chance to spend another hour with Him, even if nothing came of it.

So I cast off and headed out. I can remember John making some mocking remark, and Jesus and I just laughed. There was such joy in Him. He could be so serious at times, but the joy was always there, like bedrock at the core of His being.

Then I let out my net. I remember this part like it was yesterday. First I heard a patter against the side of the boat. When I looked over the gunwale, it was as though the water was alive, more fish than water. And as we drew the net back, I thought our little boat was going to capsize. Then the net started to tear.

I signaled back to James and John who were just loading their nets back into their father's boat, and they headed out to help us. I think we got more fish in that one afternoon outing than we had taken in the entire month before. That was the moment I fully grasped it: He was indeed Messiah. That was also the day He told us He was going to teach us to catch men.

As my thoughts wandered back to that time, some of my tension lifted—at least until I noticed the new day dawning on the horizon. We'd been out all night doing what we did best but had nothing to show for it. My funk slammed down again with such force, I thought I felt the boat shake.

Then I heard Him calling from the shore. At least I thought it was Jesus. I couldn't tell for sure, but there He stood on the shore, beside a roaring fire, signaling for us to come in. We looked at each other, and all at once we said, "It's Him! Is it you?" we called across the water.

"Drop your nets on the other side," He said from the shore. As we did, I heard it again, a patter on the side of the boat. The fish were jumping into our nets before we even got them into the water. These fish fought to get into our nets with all their might. Were they created for this moment—for this purpose?

As soon as I saw what was happening, I hit the waves and swam as hard as I could. A multitude of thoughts passed through my mind as I swam. We had spent so much of our time on the water together, back and forth across this very lake. And yet, even as I approached my dear friend, the heaviness was still there.

When I got to shore, I figured it out. As soon as we embraced, I realized what was dragging me down, what kept haunting my days and leaving my bed empty at night.

I had denied this One I loved more than I had ever loved anyone. This man had who given me three years of His life, stood alone before the Roman Empire and the Jewish power system, and I couldn't—wouldn't—even admit I knew Him.

We ate fish for breakfast—some we'd caught and some He already had on the fire. It seemed everyone around the fire that morning was exploding with joy, but I was quiet.

Jesus caught my eye and said,

"Simon."

He had given me another name, Peter, but in tender moments He still called me by my given name.

"Simon, let's walk."

As we left the group, He put His hand on my shoulder.

"Do you love me more than these?"

What was He asking? Did He want to know if I loved Him more than my fishing companions? Was He offended when we left the upper room and headed to the boats?

"Yes, Lord, you know I love you," I said with a defensive tone.

He said, *"Tend my lambs."*

We walked along the beach in silence for a few minutes.

"Simon, son of John, do you love me?"

"Yes, Lord, you know I love you."

This time He said, *"Shepherd my sheep."*

We walked along and came to a large, driftwood log. He sat down and gestured for me to join Him.

This time He almost whispered the question.

"Simon, son of John, do you Love me?"

"Yes, Lord, you know everything. You know I love you."

"Tend my sheep."

Then it all made sense. The last time we'd talked one-on-one was when He told me I would deny Him three times. Now He gave me three chances to acknowledge Him, three times to declare myself for Him.

Three failures redeemed. Three wounds healed. Three chains holding my heart, broken off and thrown into Galilee. Jesus would never speak of these three failures again. The evil one could never use these three denials to accuse me. These three sins were gone, and I was free.

As we walked back to the group, we talked of other things, but just before we reached them He said:

"Follow me."

My heart cried out, as it did the first time He said those words to me, "I will follow You."

A few minutes earlier I would have been afraid to make any promises. After all, my last failure—my last promise—ended in such disaster. But everything in me knew I would be following Him till my last day. And this time, if need be, I would die with Him.

I will gladly take up my cross and follow Jesus.

~~~

To read the original story, see John 20 and 21.

AFTERWORD

Have these stories impacted you?

What have you seen as you followed Jesus through His life, death, and resurrection?

Have you found yourself in these stories? Have you felt His healing touch? Have you heard His call to come walk on the water with Him? Were you tempted to walk away when heard Him say "…sell whatever you own…?"

Much of what you have read is fiction—my imagination—but I hope and pray you can hear the voice of the Spirit in these stories calling you to the cross and to the Savior.

For many of you, this has been a walk with the One you know and love as Savior and Lord, and I hope it has come to life for you in a new way.

But if you have never given your life to Jesus, I want to offer you that opportunity right now. Jesus is the one—foretold for centuries— who came to the world He created, walked the streets of Palestine, died a criminal's death, bearing the sin of every man and woman. He was tempted in the same ways we are, yet never yielded to sin.

Here's the deal. He doesn't ask you to add Him to your already busy life. He doesn't ask you to join a church and give Him some of your money. He asks you to take up your cross and follow Him. Jesus is not an add-on to your life. As the one who created you, He asks to be your Master and Lord, your friend and companion.

If you will surrender your life to Him today, He will come and live in you. Does that sound crazy? It's true. The One who created all things will come by His Spirit and live in you. He'll never leave you alone. He'll walk with you as He walked with those you read about in this book.

Will you tell me how this book has impacted you? I would love to know. You can contact me via email at: Ben@AnotherRedLetterDay.com.

~~~

If you would like to use one or more of these stories to punctuate a service or ministry time, please do. We have used a number of them, either read dramatically or presented in character, to enhance Sunday services, Bible studies, and other events. Feel free to tweak them to fit your needs. I would ask that you credit the book and share information on how those interested might obtain a copy.

If you're interested in having me speak or share at your event, contact me via email at: Ben@AnotherRedLetterDay.com